Drag and Drop
E-Mail

Davinder Singh Minhas

STERLING PUBLISHERS PVT. LTD.
A-59, Okhla Industrial Area, Phase-II, New Delhi
Ph.: 26386165, 26387070, 26386209
Fax: 91-11-26383788
E-mail: mail@sterlingpublishers.com
Website: www.sterlingpublishers.com

ISBN: 978-81-207-5734-9
© 2011, E-mail
All rights reserved. No part of this publication may be reproduced, stored in a retrieval system, or transmitted, in any form or by any means, electronic, mechanical, photocopying, recording or otherwise, without the prior permission of the original publishers.

Printed at Sterling Publishers Private Limited., New Delhi-110020. India

Contents

Introduction	5
Features of e-mail	11
Sending and receiving e-mail	16
Outlook 2010	21
Hotmail account	34

1 Introduction

E-mail is the short form of **e**lectronic **m**ail. It is a transmission of messages and file via communication networks, such as a local area network or the Internet, usually between computers. Today, e-mail enables administrators, teachers and students to communicate with millions of Internet users all over the world. It has become the fastest and cheapest way to exchange text and messages.

ELECTRONIC MAIL

People have been using various means to communicate with each other for thousands of years.

Fire was used as a means of communication in many parts of the world. In 1588, a chain of bonfires was used to send warning signals from one end of the country to the other. In India, kings and emperors stationed relay horses to send messages from one part to another.

Pigeons have been used to send letters and messages from time immemorial.

In **AD** 1, the first postal service was started by China, Persia and the Roman Empire. Messages were written on scrolls and carried on horse-backs, or by ships. In such cases, messages would take weeks to arrive because of the long distances. Later, armed mail coaches were used. The mail started being sent by train in the 19th century, making the postal service much cheaper to use. The first air mail service began in 1918, between Washington DC and New York. Letters and packages could be sent across the two cities in just two days.

Drag and Drop Series

In 1837, the messages could be sent over long distances very quickly with the invention of the telegraph. A telegraph message could travel between the continents in a few minutes.

Ray Tomlinson developed the first email application for the ARPANET in 1971, consisting of a program called SNDMSG for sending mail, and a program called READMAIL for reading mail. In the 1980s messages were exchanged between computers in offices and universities that had been linked together. By 1990, e-mail had gone global and had evolved as the most efficient means of communication.

The number of e-mail users and e-mail messages has grown phenomenally during the past few years, as indicated by this graph.

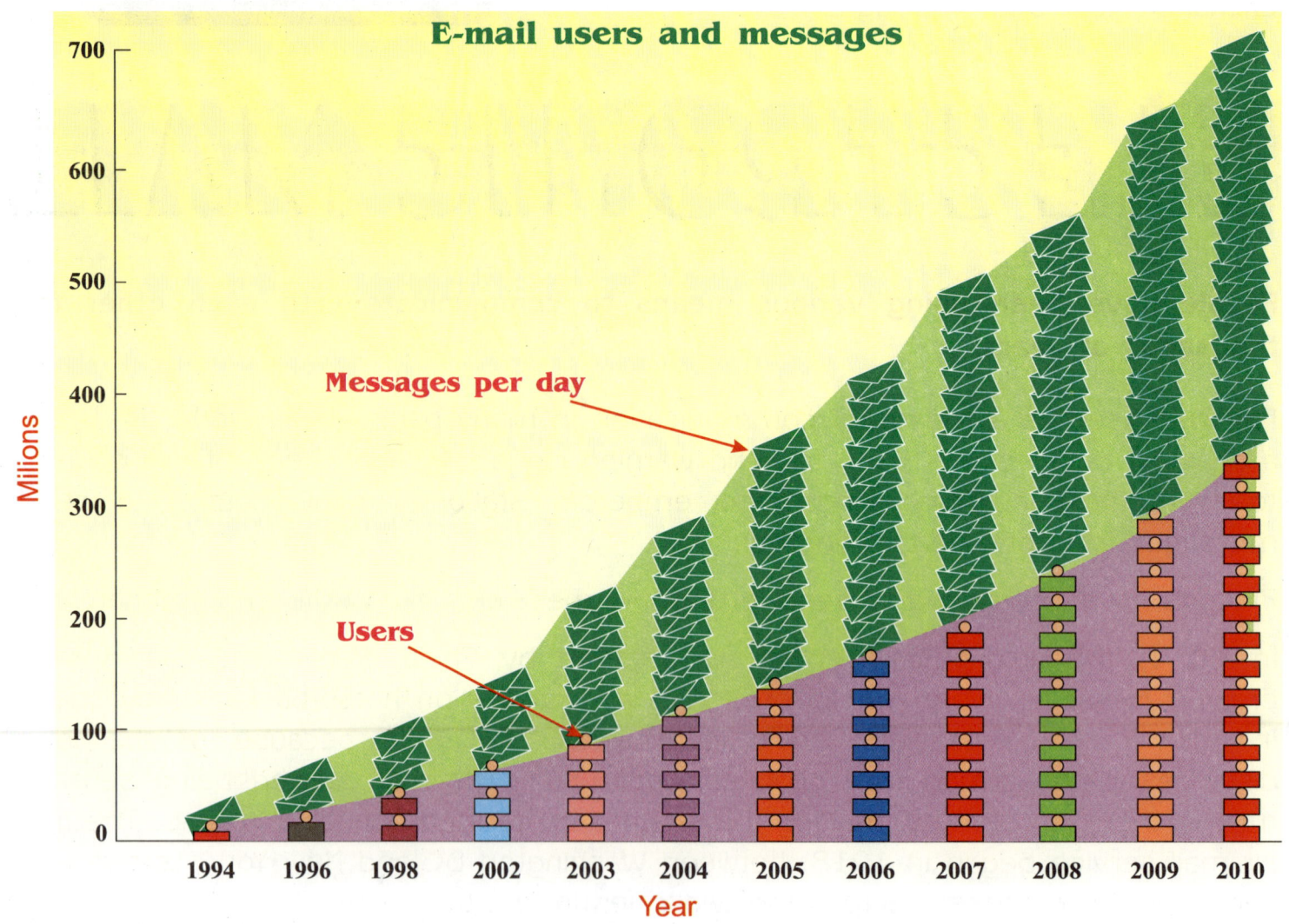

Now, let us look at an example to compare the process of sending a message via the **Internet** or by **sending a letter by post**.

E-mail

Just type the address, compose your message and press the **Send** button.

Sending a letter by ordinary post

First get a headed notepaper, find an envelope, go to the Post Office to buy the stamps, write the letter, put it in an envelope and go to the postbox to drop the letter.

Simple mail could take a day, or two days, (or three or...) for the post to arrive, whereas the e-mail could be delivered in a matter of seconds, or a few minutes.

SOME ADVANTAGES OF E-MAIL

1. E-mail is extremely fast. One can receive a message in a matter of seconds after it has been sent, irrespective of the geographic location of the sender and the recipient. You cannot find a better medium than the e-mail.

2. When you send an e-mail message, the person you send it to does not have to be on the computer at that time to receive it. The mail can be collected whenever the person chooses to log on to his computer network or mail server.

3. You can send a message to a group of people at a low cost, as quickly and easily as you can send to one person.

4. You can send documents, graphics, sound files, or any file as an attachment along with your e-mail.

5. There is no charge for sending and receiving e-mail, the only charge you need to pay is to your Service Provider. There is no extra payment even if a long message is sent or the message has to travel to the remotest corner of the world.

E-MAIL PROGRAMS

An e-mail program is used to create, send, receive, forward, store, print, and delete messages. When you receive an e-mail message, your Internet Service Provider's software places the message in your personal **mailbox**. Your mailbox is a storage location usually residing on the computer that connects you to the Internet, such as the server operated by your ISP. A server that contains the user's mailboxes and associated e-mail messages is called a **Mail Server**.

The two of the most popular e-mail programs are **Outlook Express** and **Hotmail**.

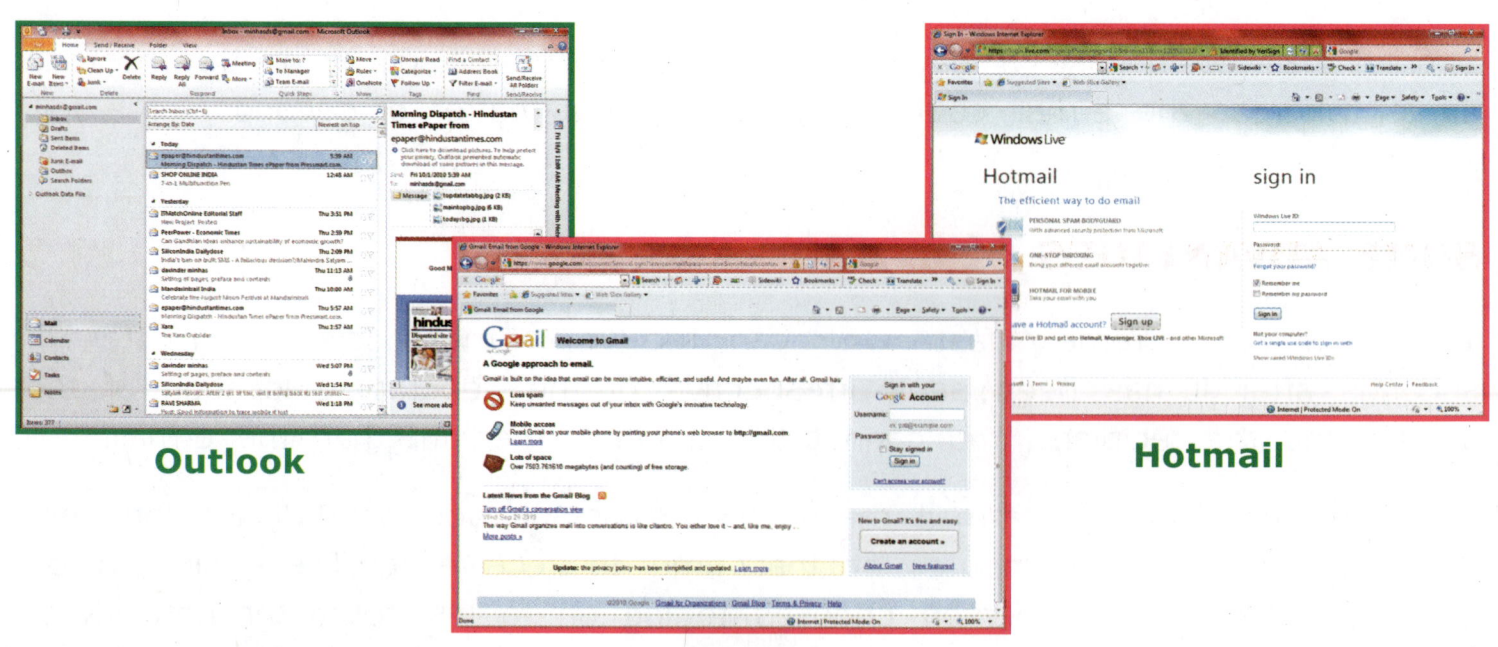

Outlook   **Gmail**   **Hotmail**

HOW E-MAIL TRAVELS

The computers have to be linked together so that the e-mail message can travel.

1. An e-mail message is typed by the sender on his computer.

2. The message has an address, so that it can be sent directly to the right address.

3. The message is sent to a server which is connected to the Internet.

4. The e-mail is then sent to a router by the server. The first router sends the message to another router. Routers are connected to each other by telephone lines and cables.

5. The message is sent from one router to another until it reaches at the correct one.

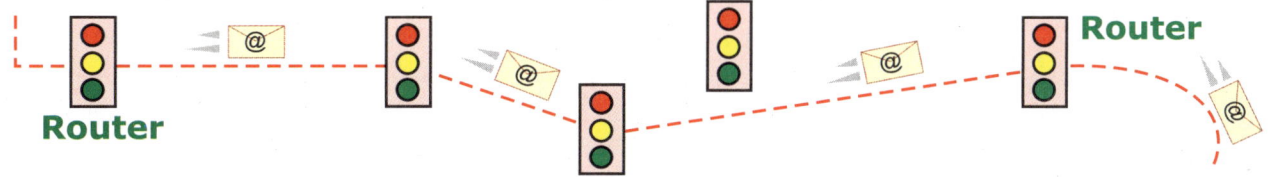

6. The e-mail is finally passed by the router to the server. When the recipient's computer is connected to the server, the message can be displayed.

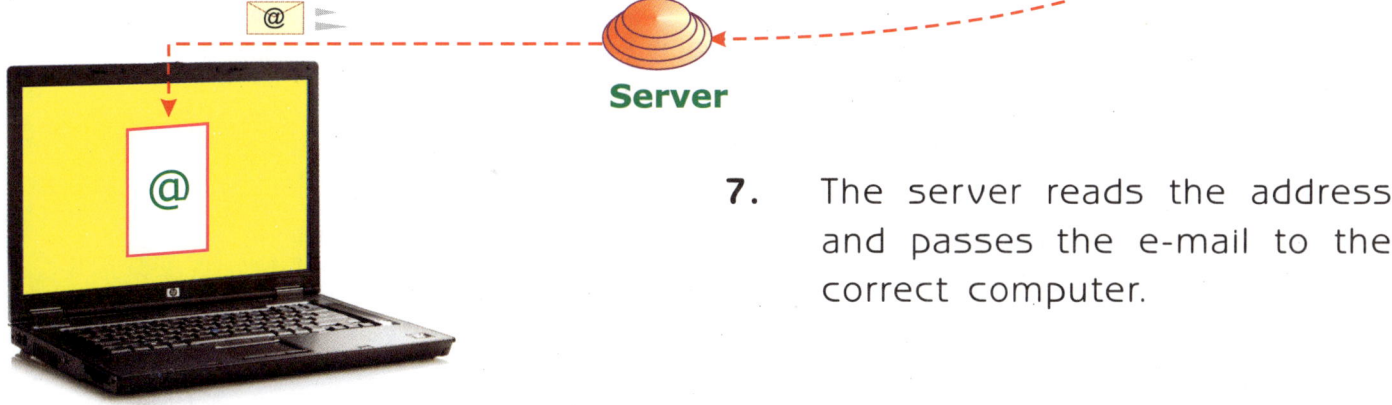

7. The server reads the address and passes the e-mail to the correct computer.

Sometimes routers are too busy, or not working. In such cases, the e-mail messages are sent via other working routers.

HOW COMPUTERS EXCHANGE INFORMATION

You need to have a set of rules like **protocol**, which determines how the information is to be sent. **I**nternet **P**rotocol (IP) is the most important protocol used on the Net. It specifies that the information sent between computers, servers and routers must be broken down into 'packets' of data.

WHAT ARE PACKETS?

Packets are the small chunks which are broken by the Net while sending the e-mail message from one computer to another. Each packet contains the address of the destination computer. The messages are put back together to form the e-mail message, when this message reaches the designated computer.

2 Features of e-mail

E-MAIL ADDRESS

If you have an e-mail address, you can send e-mail messages anywhere in the world. All e-mail users have their own, unique e-mail address. The messages are sent to the right computer because of the uniqueness of the address.

Parts of an e-mail address

An **e-mail address** is a combination of a user name and a domain name that identifies the user so he or she can receive messages. Your **user name** is a unique combination of characters that identifies you, and it must differ from other user names located on the same mail server. **Domain name** is the location of the person's account on the Internet.

An e-mail address consists of two parts (User name and Domain name) separated by the @ symbol. @ means at.

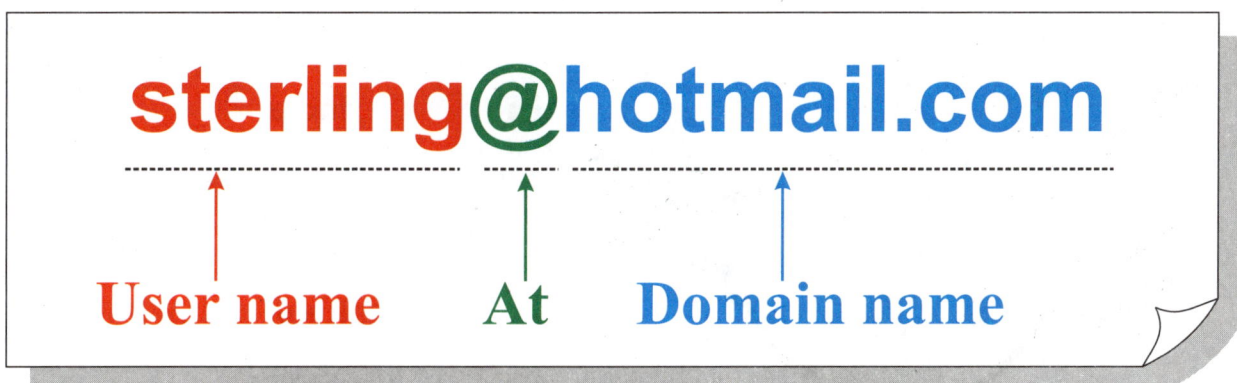

An e-mail address cannot have commas, spaces or brackets. Instead, hyphens and underscores can be used.

Drag and Drop Series

DOMAIN NAME

The **domain name** is separated into two parts by the period (.), and it is the location of the person's account on the Internet.

Types of domain name

The last few characters in an e-mail address shows the kind of organization the domain belongs to. These characters also shows the name of the country a person belongs to.

Organization

com	commercial
edu	education
gov	government
mil	military
net	network
org	organization

Country

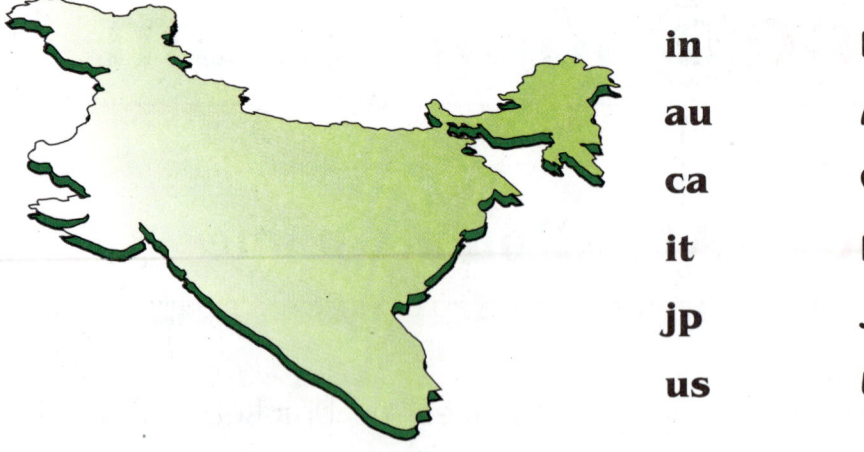

in	India
au	Australia
ca	Canada
it	Italy
jp	Japan
us	United States

SELECTING AN E-MAIL ADDRESS

While creating an e-mail account the server will let you choose a user name. Your user name should be separate and has to be a name that hasn't already been chosen by anyone else. So, it is recommended that you use a combination of letters and numbers.

For example, a user Rahul Bajaj, whose server has a domain name of hotmail.com, might select r_bajaj as his user name. If hotmail.com already has r_bajaj (for Rajiv Bajaj), Rahul would have to select a different user name, such as rahulbajaj or rahul_bajaj. Many users select a combination of their first and last names so that others can remember it easily.

FINDING AN E-MAIL ADDRESS

The e-mail addresses of friends or colleagues can be found with the help of web sites. Although there is no central listing of e-mail addresses, there are many places on the web that help you search for e-mail addresses. One of the popular web site is **people.yahoo.com**

PARTS OF AN E-MAIL MESSAGE

An e-mail message has several parts like From:, To:, Cc:, Bcc: and Subject. When you are in the process of writing an e-mail message these are the parts that you come across.

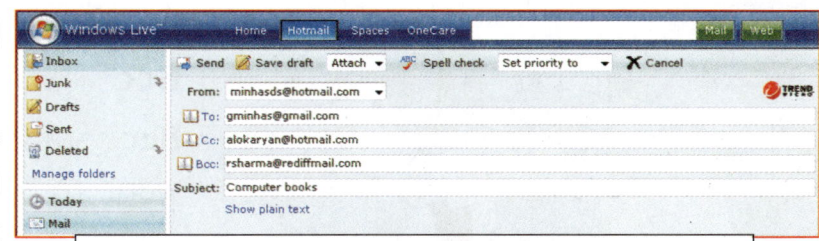

From: minhasds@hotmail.com
To: gminhas@gmail.com
Cc: alokaryan@hotmail.com
Bcc: rsharma@rediffmail.com
Subject: Computer Books

Please send me the detail of your computer books.

Thank you,
With Regards,
Davinder Singh Minhas

From

The person who is sending the e-mail message writes his/her e-mail address in this section.

To

The address of the person to whom the mail is being sent, is written here.

Cc

Cc stands for **carbon copy**. It is an exact copy of the message that you have typed. The address of a person who is not directly involved with the message but you would like to keep in the loop, goes here.

Bcc

Bcc stands for **blind carbon copy**. If you want to send the same message to several people, you can type their addresses here.

Subject

The summary of your message is written in this section. For example if you are sending a resume in your e-mail, you can write Resume in the Subject section.

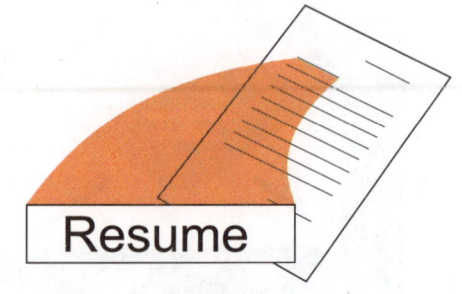

FEATURES OF AN E-MAIL PROGRAM

New message

Clicking on this button allows you to write a new e-mail to someone by invoking the e-mail authoring program.

Reply

This button will allow you to send a reply to someone who sent you an e-mail.

Reply to all

Sometimes you can receive an email of which you are not the only recipient. Pressing this button allows you to reply to all of the email addresses in that e-mail.

Forward

This button will help you forward a message that you have received, to someone else.

Send and receive

Clicking on this button will serve two functions. It will send a query your mail server and receive any new e-mail that might be waiting for you, and it will send any pending messages, that you have authored, to your e-mail server.

Delete

This button allows you to delete the selected message.

Print

Some times you might want to keep a hand copy of the e-mail message with you. In such a situation the **Print** button allows you to take a printout of the e-mail, if the system is connected to a printer.

Organize messages

E-mail programs usually store messages that you have sent, received and deleted in separate folders. This helps you to keep messages organized so you can review them later. You can also create personalized folders to better organize your messages.

3 Sending and receiving e-mail

RECEIVING AN E-MAIL MESSAGE

Your e-mail messages can be received any time whether your computer is turned on or not. If your computer is not on at the time of receiving the mail, your Internet Service Provider will store the messages in the mailbox for you. Whenever you turn on your computer, you will get your message from the mailbox.

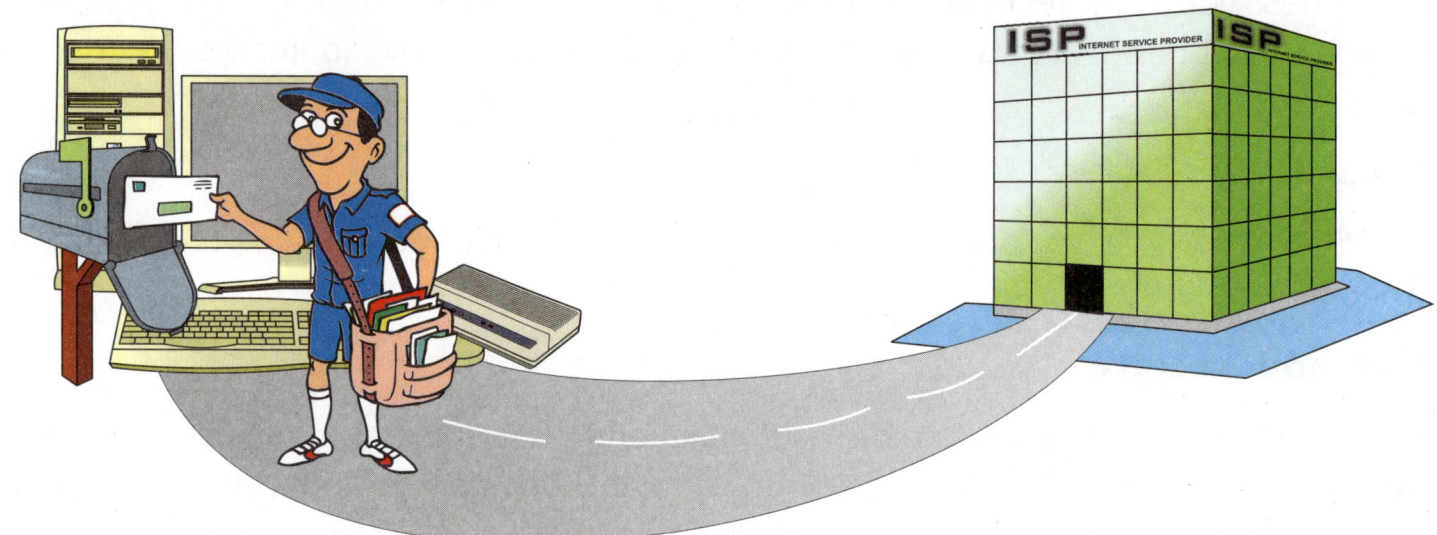

Whenever you check your new messages, you will not be checking the message directly from your computer, but from the mailbox of the service provider's computer, through your computer. That is why you can check your mail from anywhere, whether from your computer at home or from the computer of a friend in some other part of the country. This also allows you to check your messages while traveling.

Check your message regularly

You should check your messages regularly, if possible, and delete the unnecessary ones because if your mailbox gets too full, some of your messages may be deleted by your service provider or there is a possibility of getting new messages very late.

e-mail

SENDING AN E-MAIL MESSAGE

To reply to a mail that you have received or for exchanging ideas, you can send an e-mail message.

Composing an e-mail message

There are some common e-mail terms that you will come across while composing the message.

You can use your keyboard to type in a message in the message window. Click on the message box with the mouse. A flashing insertion point will appear which indicates where any character you type will appear.

If you make any mistake while typing a character, you can delete or remove the character by pressing the **Delete** key or **Backspace** key.

You can also edit your text by adding or deleting the character. It is done by moving the flashing insertion point (cursor) to any place on the message. The insertion point can be moved with the help of the arrow keys.

Drag and Drop Series

Formatting text

You can change the style and size of the text in most of e-mail programs.

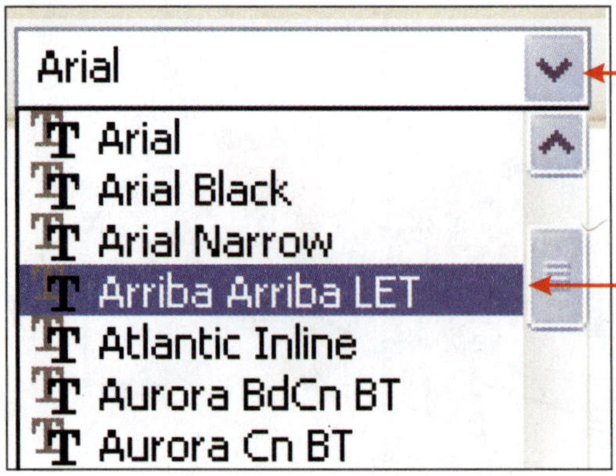

Change Font: Select the text of which you want to change the font.

1. Click on the down arrow beside the font box. A list of choices will appear.

2. Choose the style of font you want and then click on it.

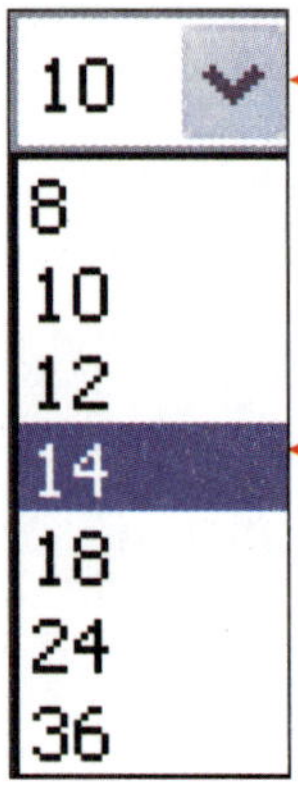

Change Font Size: Select the text of which you want to change the font size.

1. Click on the down arrow beside the font size box. A list of sizes will appear.

2. Choose the size of font you want and then click on it.

You should compose your e-mail message when you are not connected to the Internet or in offline position. After composing your messages, you can connect to the Internet and send the messages all at once.

Smileys

Also called an **emoticon**, it is an expression of emotion typed into a message using standard keyboard characters. These characters look like human faces when you turn them sideways.

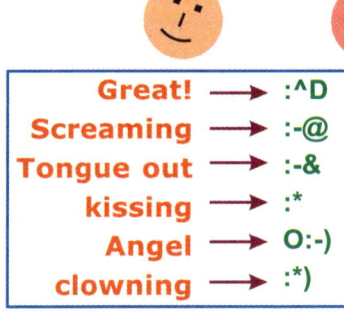

Cry → :'-(	Great! → :^D
Smile → :-)	Screaming → :-@
Laugh → :-D	Tongue out → :-&
Sad → :-(	kissing → :*
Wow → :-o	Angel → O:-)
Wink → ;-)	clowning → :*)

Abbreviation

Abbreviations are commonly used as shorthand in e-mails. They are used to save time while typing.

AISI	As I See It.	**BTW**	By The Way
AS	Another Subject.	**CU**	See You
ASAP	As Soon As Possible	**DK**	Don't Know
B4N	Bye For Now	**IC**	I See
BAK	Back At Keyboard	**LY**	Love You.
BBIAB	Be Back In A Bit.	**LOL**	Laughing Out Loud
BBL	Be Back Later	**SYS**	See You Soon.
BF	Boy Friend.	**Gr8**	Great

Shouting

To use ALL CAPITAL LETTERS in an e-mail is annoying and very hard to read. This is called shouting. A word can be more acceptably emphasized by placing it between *asterisks* or _underscores_. E-mail messages should always use upper and lower case letters.

Please Don't Shout

Bounced messages

A bounced message is a message informing the user that an e-mail could not be delivered to its intended recipients. The failure may be due to an incorrectly typed e-mail address or a network problem.

Signature

Signature is a pre-written text file appended to the end of an e-mail message that is used as a closing or an end to the message. It typically contains the sender's name and address, but may contain any kind of text that is repetitively sent.

Drag and Drop Series

Address book

In the e-mail program, the Address Book is a utility that enables users to store and retrieve e-mail address and other contact information. It saves you from having to type the same address over and over again.

Attachment

A file (or group of files) that is included (or 'attached') with an e-mail message is called an **'Attachment'**. Usually, this is accomplished by simply clicking on the **attach file** button and then browsing through your computer system to find and select the desired file or image.

E-MAIL VIRUS

Virus is a potentially damaging computer program, which negatively affects or infects your computer without your knowledge and alters the working of the computer. Most viruses are harmless, but some can be destructive. The increased use of e-mail has accelerated the spread of computer viruses. With these technologies, computer users can easily share files and any related viruses along with it.

One of the most common way of a virus entering your computer is through the attachment in an e-mail. Before you open or execute any e-mail attachment, you should ensure that the e-mail message is from a trusted source. A **trusted source** is a company or a person you believe will not send you a virus-infected file knowingly. You should immediately delete any e-mail received from an unknown source without opening or executing the attachment. Thus, you can protect your computer against viruses.

Virus scanner

A virus scanner is an anti-virus program that you can use to check e-mail attachments for viruses. Virus scanner manufacturers regularly release updates that allow their programs to detect the latest known viruses. Always make sure your virus scanner is up-to-date.

4 Outlook 2010

Outlook is an e-mail program which has been developed by Microsoft. You can create, send, receive, forward, store, print and delete messages using an e-mail program.

OPENING AN E-MAIL ACCOUNT IN OUTLOOK

Outlook is an e-mail program which comes with MS-Office. You can check your mail and send replies by opening your mail account with Outlook.

Follow these steps to open your mail account:

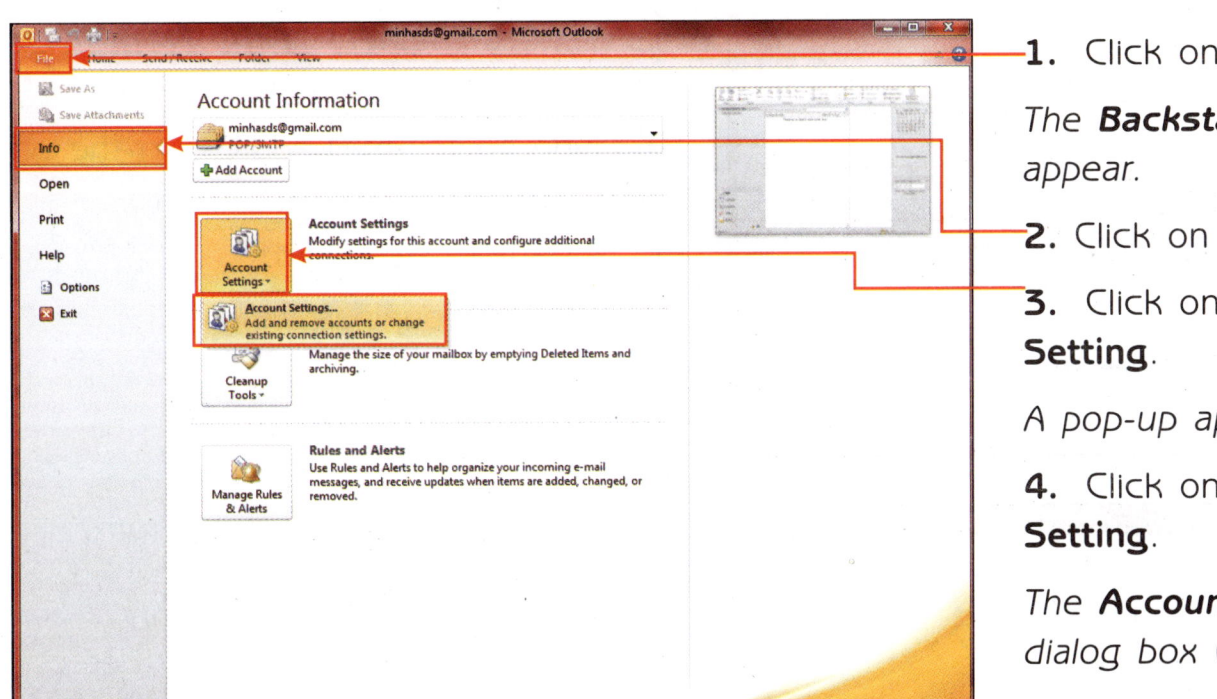

1. Click on **File** button.

   The **Backstage view** will appear.

2. Click on **Info**.

3. Click on **Account Setting**.

   A pop-up appears.

4. Click on **Account Setting**.

   The **Accounts Settings** dialog box will appear.

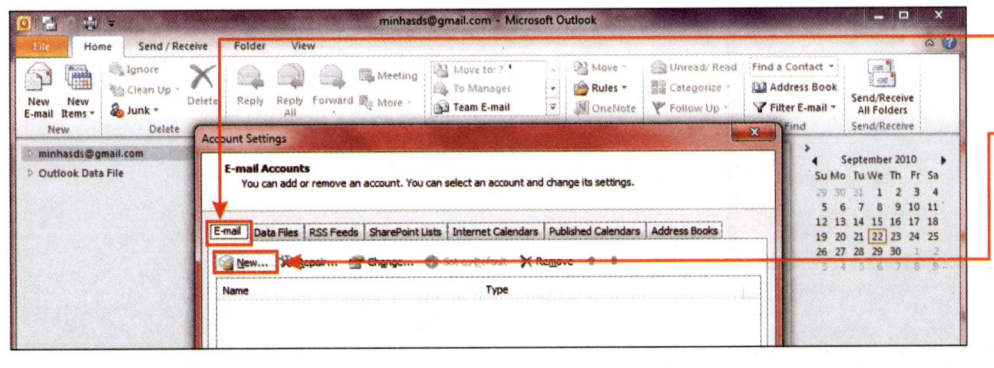

5. Click on the **E-mail** tab.

6. Click on the **New** button to start a new account.

Drag and Drop Series

The **Add New Account** wizard will appear.

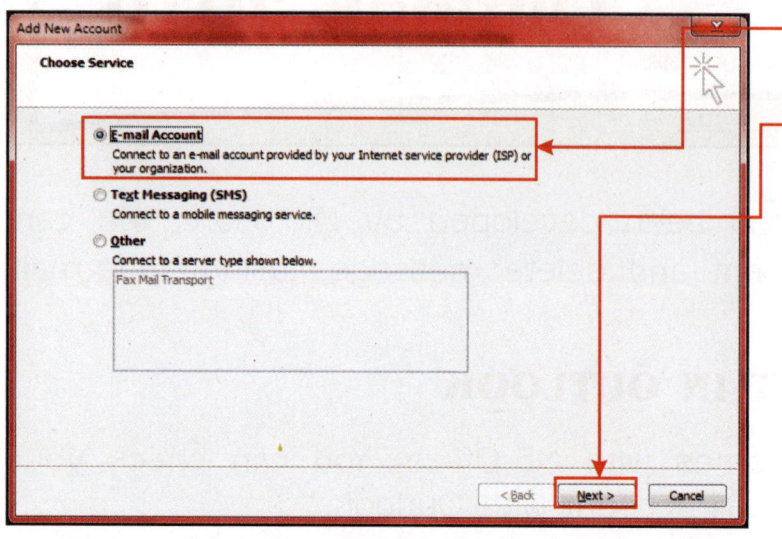

7. Click on the radio button of **E-mail Account**.

8. Click on **Next**.

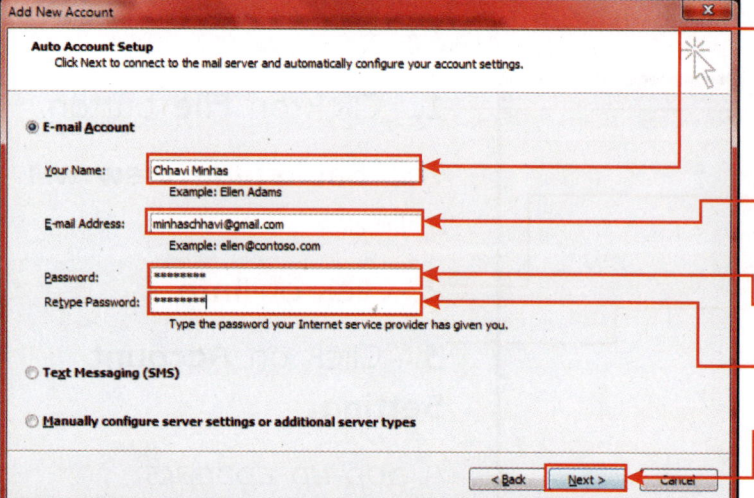

9. Type your name in this area.

   *This name will appear in the **From** field of the outgoing mail.*

10. Type your e-mail address in the **E-mail address** text box.

11. Type your password.

12. Re-type your password.

13. Click on **Next**.

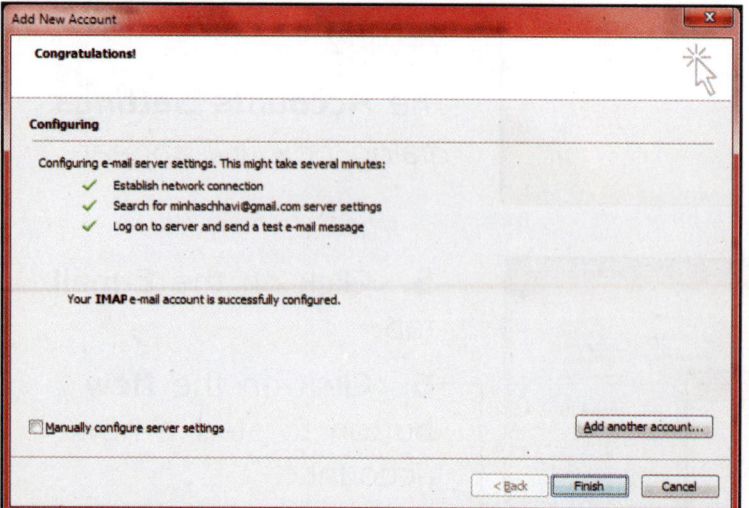

If you are using mail services from Microsoft such as Windows Live Hotmail, G-mail or pop3 account, Outlook 2010 will automatically detect your e-mail server settings.

14. Click on **Finish**.

e-mail

But, if you are not using any e-mail services from Microsoft you will need to configure your server settings manually. To do this, you can click the check box of **Manually configure server settings or additional server types**.

Configure server settings manually

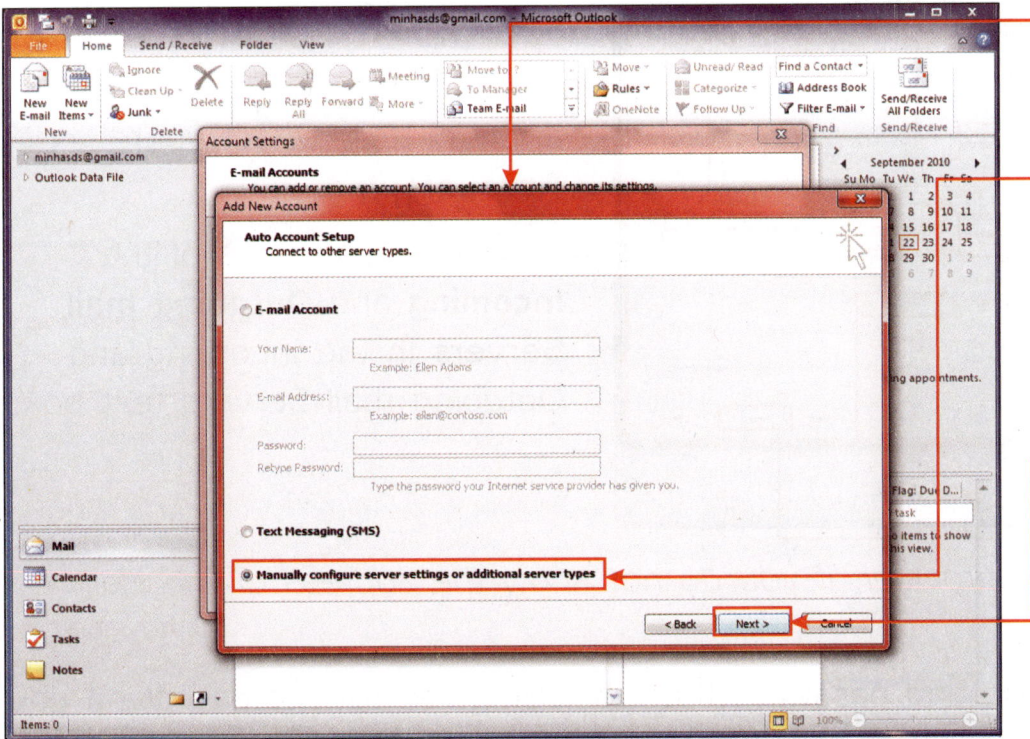

1. Repeat steps 1 - **8**, the **Add New Account** wizard will appear.

2. Click on the check box of **Manually configure server settings or additional server types.**

3. Click on **Next**.

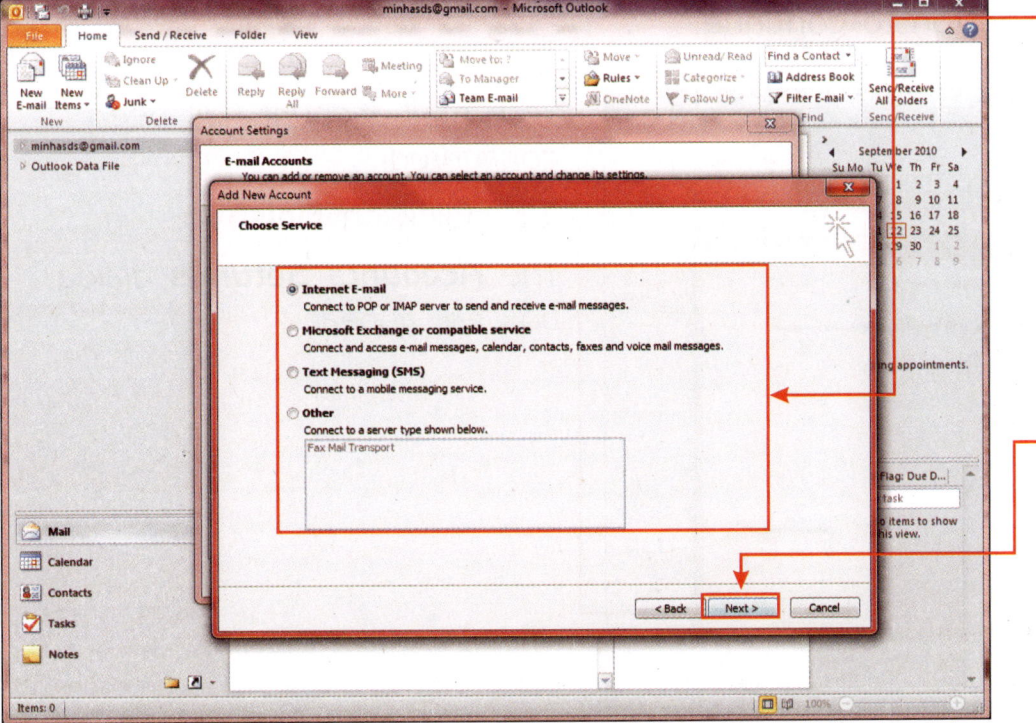

4. Click on the radio button of the type of mail server your e-mail service is using.

In this example we are using the first option - Internet E-mail (POP, IMAP or HTTP).

5. Click on **Next**.

23

Drag and Drop Series

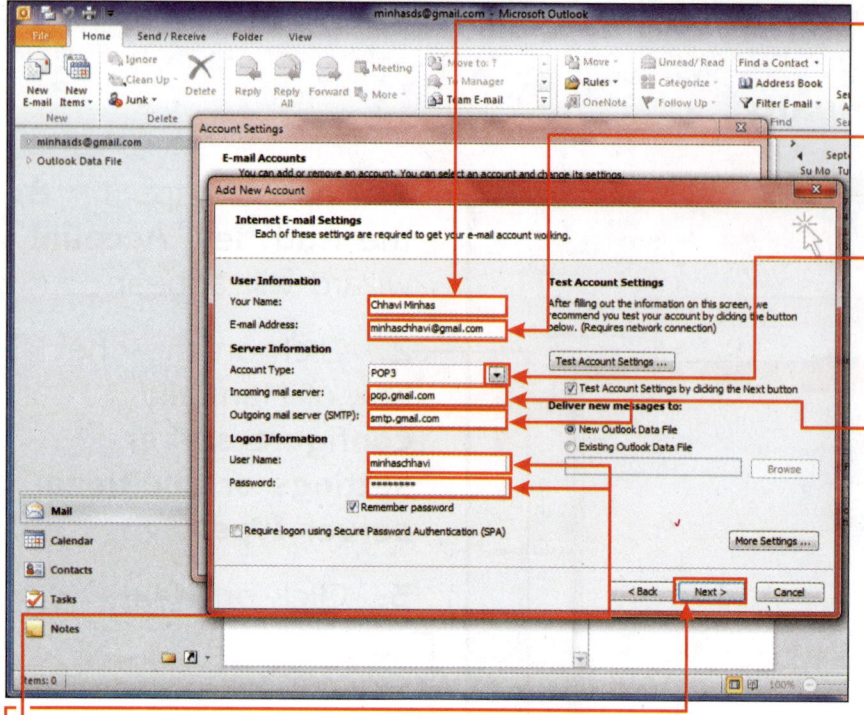

6. Type your name in this area.

7. Type your **e-mail address** in E-mail address text box.

8. By clicking on the down arrow button, select your **Account Type**.

9. Type the address of the **Incoming** and **Outgoing mail Servers** in the Incoming and Outgoing mail Servers text box.

Note: Contact your Mail provider, if you do not know the address of the Mail Servers.

10. Type the User name and password that your Service Provider has given you in the **User Name** and **Password** text box.

11. Click on the **Next** button to continue.

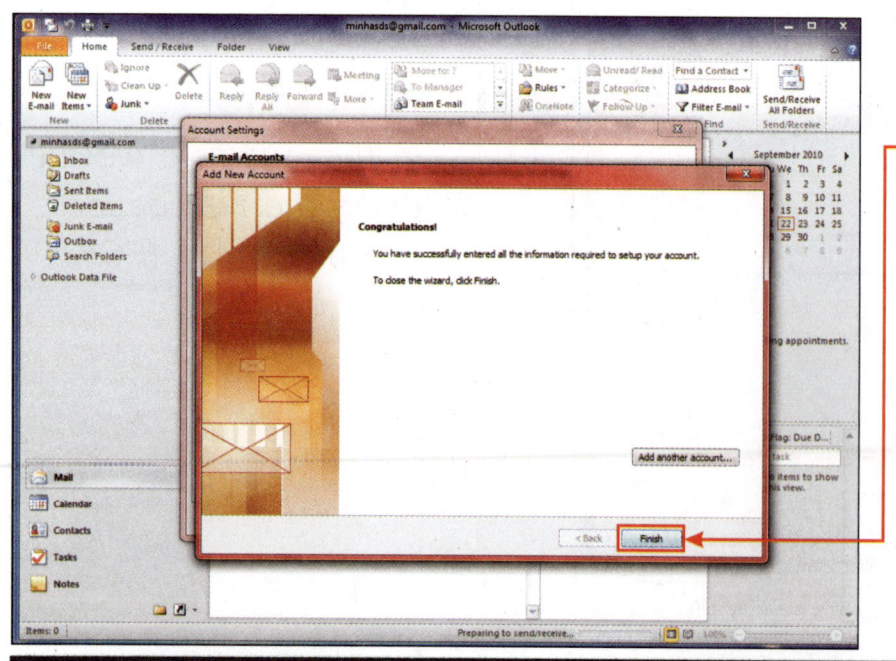

Your mail account has been configured.

12. Click on **Finish** button.

The **Accounts Settings** dialog box will appear.

e-mail

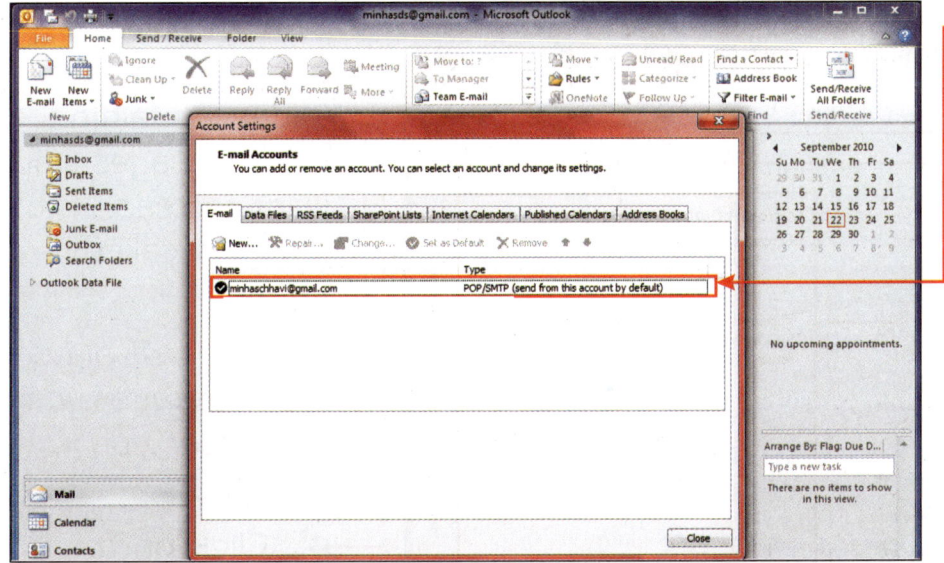

Your new e-mail account appears in this area.

READING AND EXCHANGING MAILS

To open and read the contents of your e-mail messages, you can start Outlook.

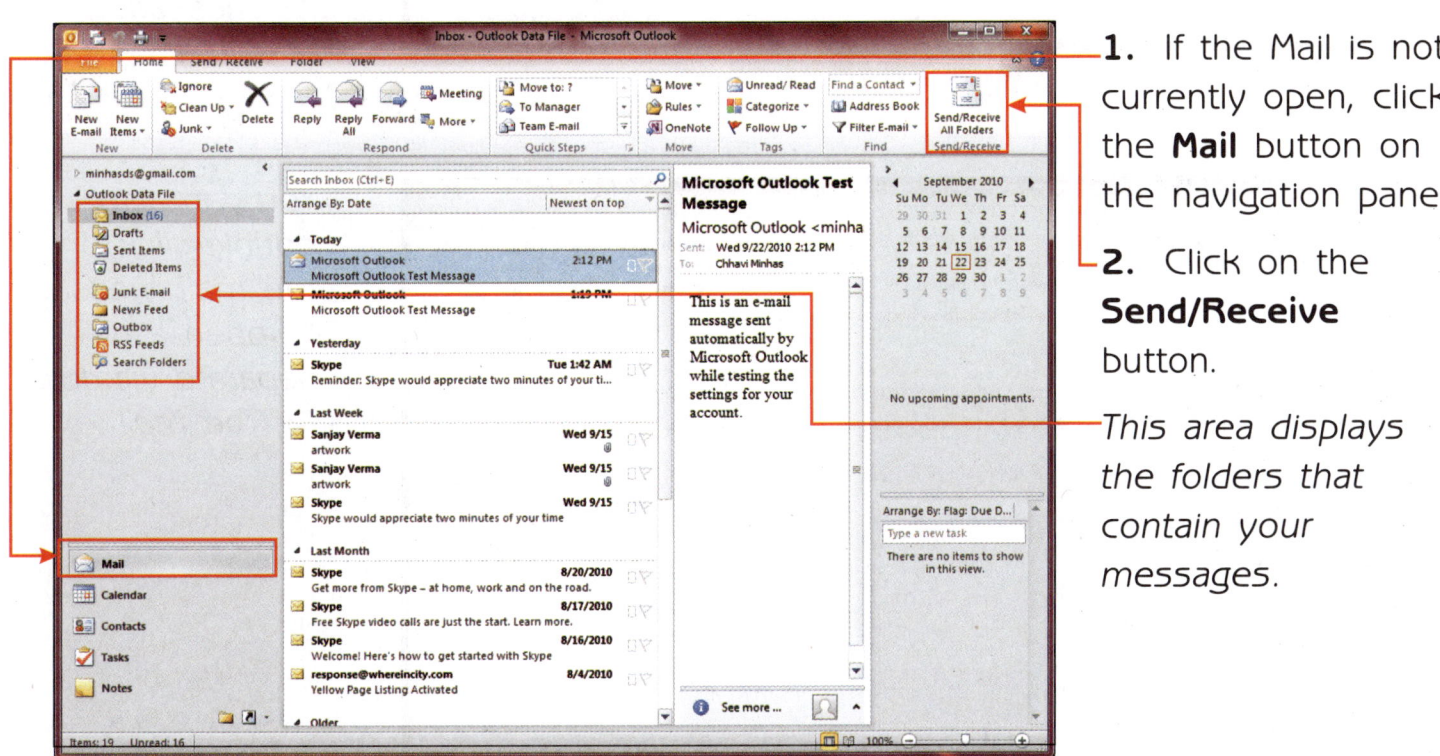

1. If the Mail is not currently open, click the **Mail** button on the navigation pane.

2. Click on the **Send/Receive** button.

This area displays the folders that contain your messages.

A number in brackets beside a folder indicates how many unread messages the folder contains. The number disappears when you have read all the messages in the folder.

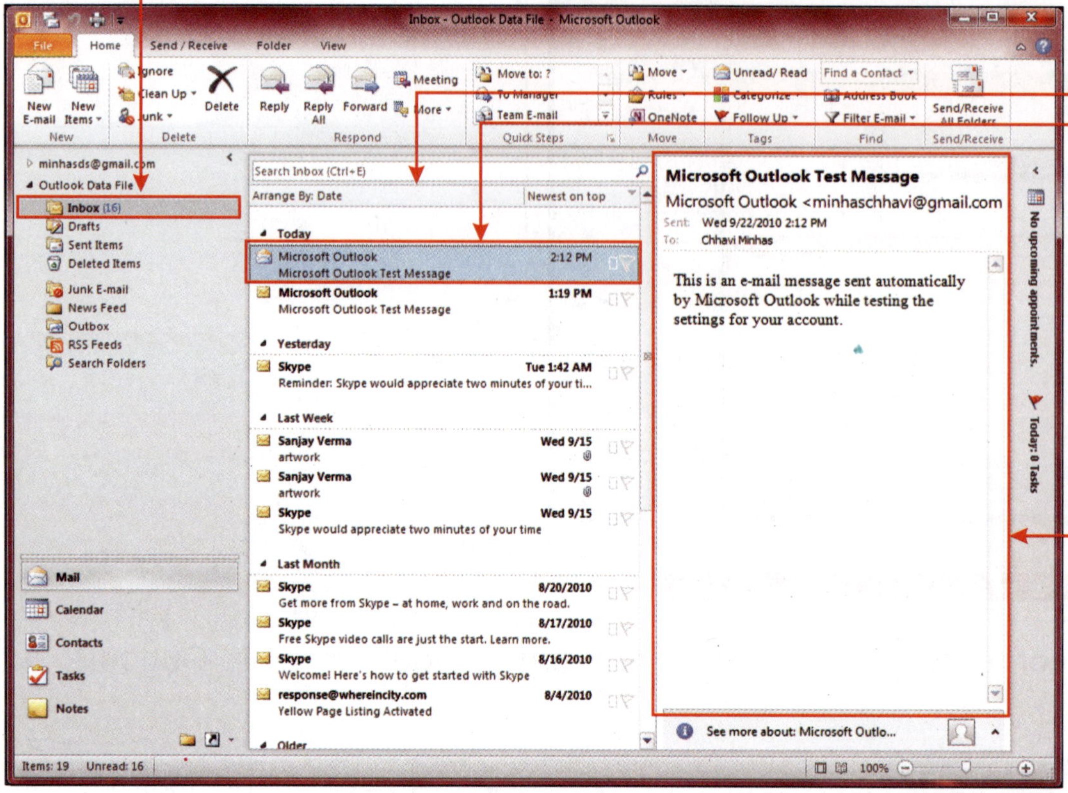

Drag and Drop Series

3. Click on the folder containing the messages you want to read. The folder is called **Inbox**.

This area displays the messages in the folder you selected.

4. Click on a message you want to read.

This area displays the contents of the message.

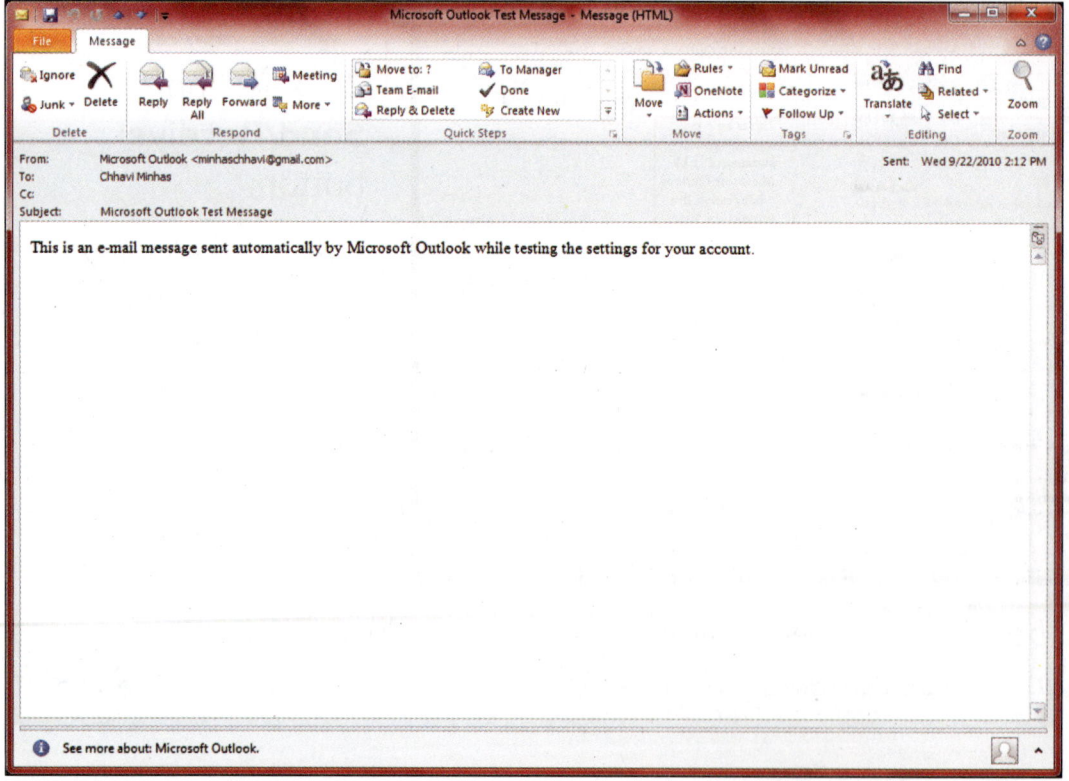

You can also double-click on the mail message to open a separate window for the mail.

e-mail

PREVIEW AND OPEN ATTACHMENT

If you receive a message with a file attached to it, you can use Outlook to quickly preview the contents of the attached file in the reading pane. Attachments are identified by a special paperclip icon.

Preview an attachment

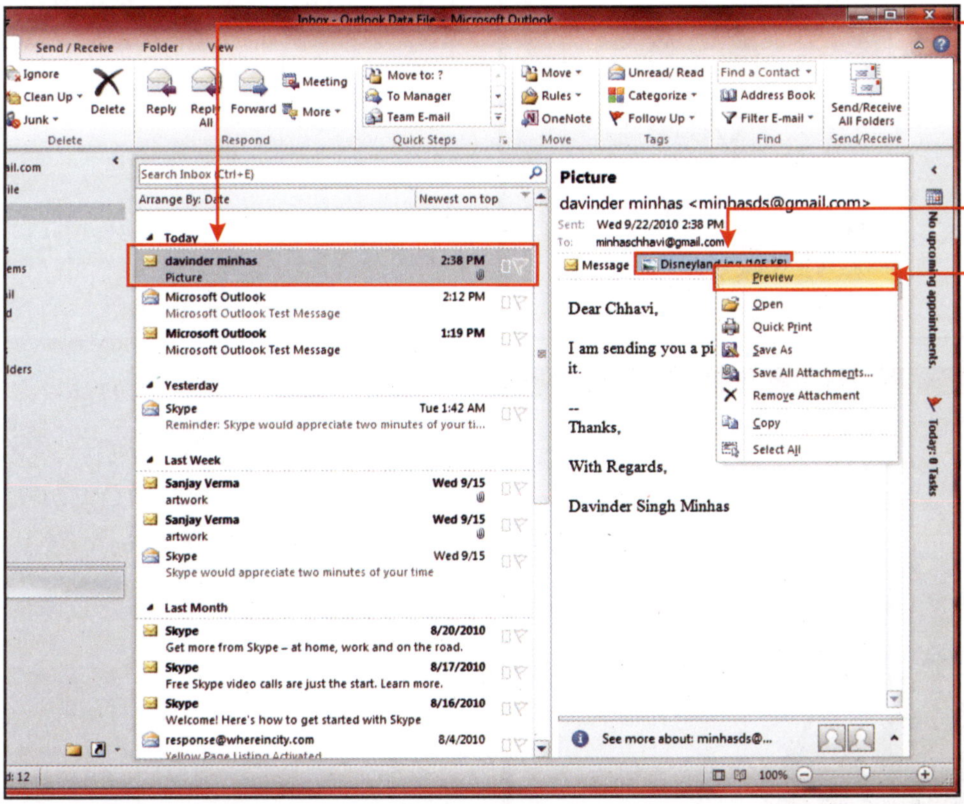

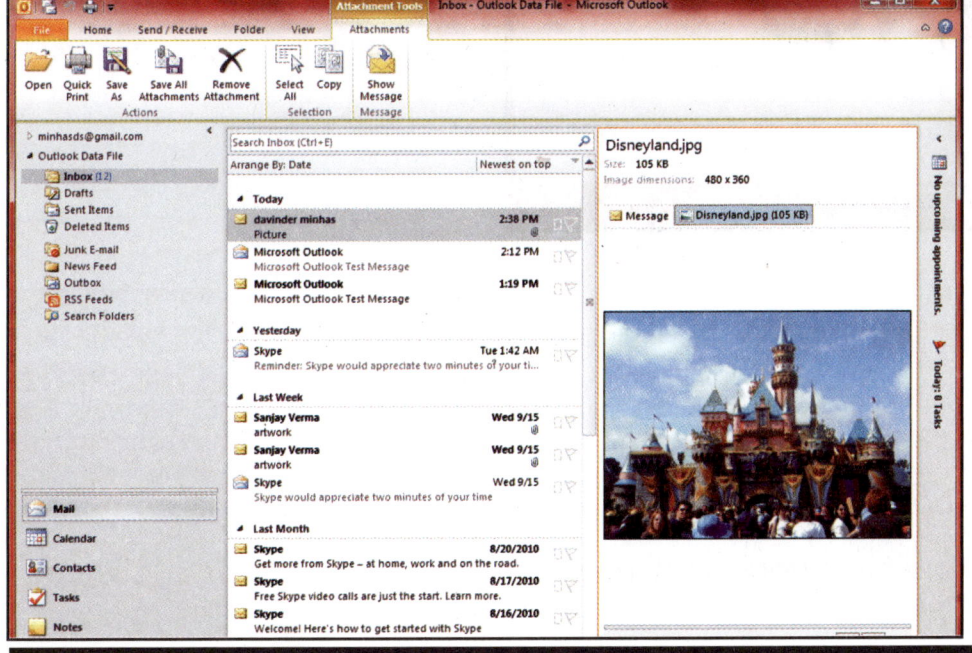

1. Click on the message that contains an attachment.

   The message's contents are displayed.

2. Right-click the attachment.

3. Click on **Preview**.

The contents of the attachment appear in the reading pane.

27

Drag and Drop Series

Opening an attachment

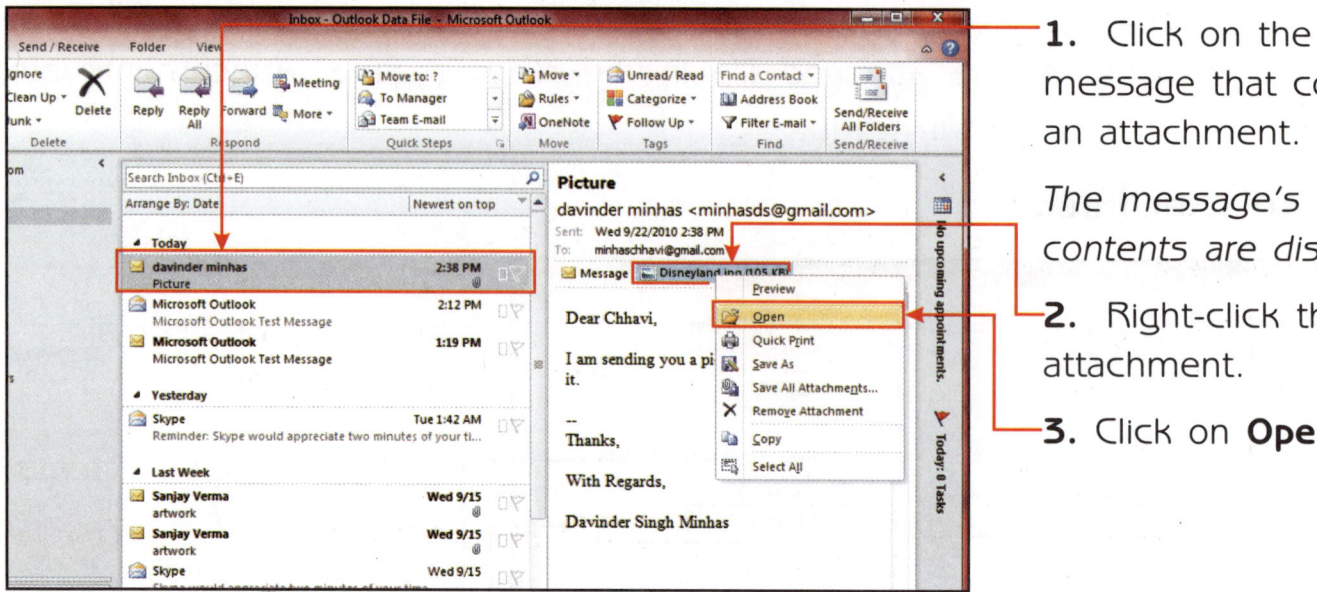

1. Click on the message that contains an attachment.

The message's contents are displayed.

2. Right-click the attachment.

3. Click on **Open**.

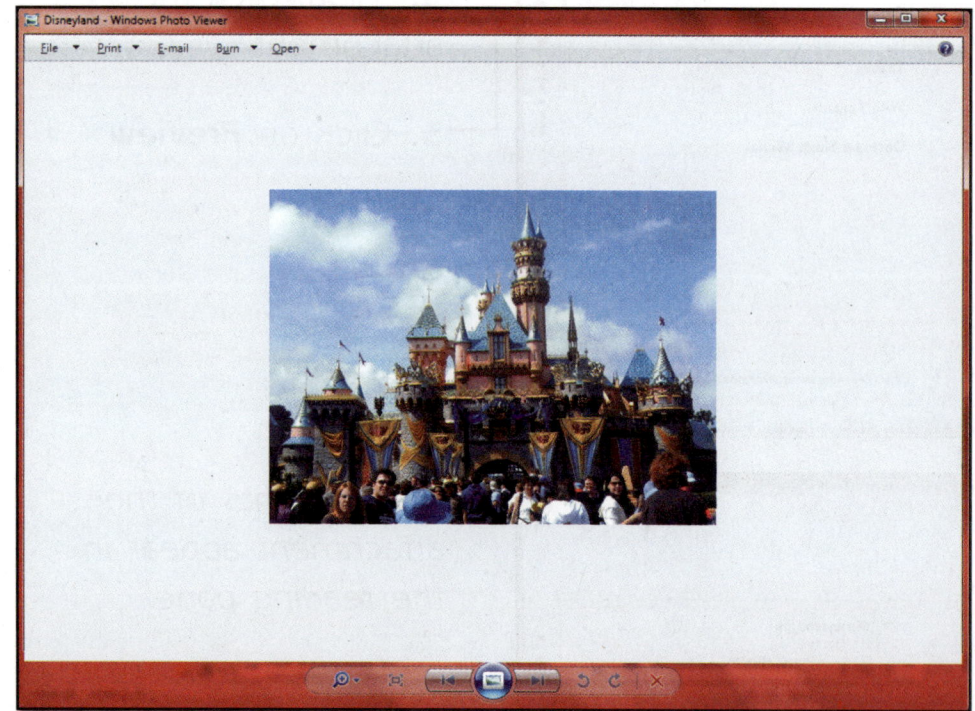

The file opens in the appropriate program (assuming that program is installed on your PC).

Saving an attachment

1. Repeat steps **1** and **2**.

2. Click on **Save as**.

The **Save Attachment** dialog box appears.

Locate and select the folder in which you want to save the file and click on **Save**.

e-mail

SENDING A MESSAGE

A message can be sent to express an idea or request for some information.

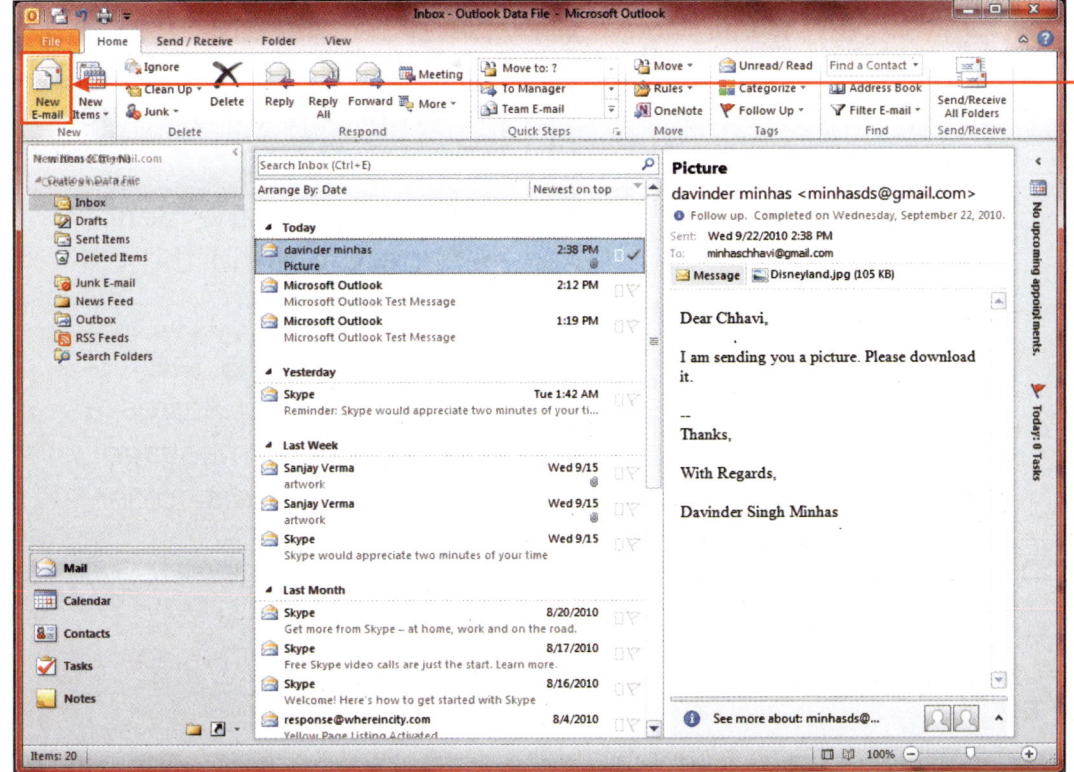

1. Click on **New** to send a new message.

   The **New Message** window appears.

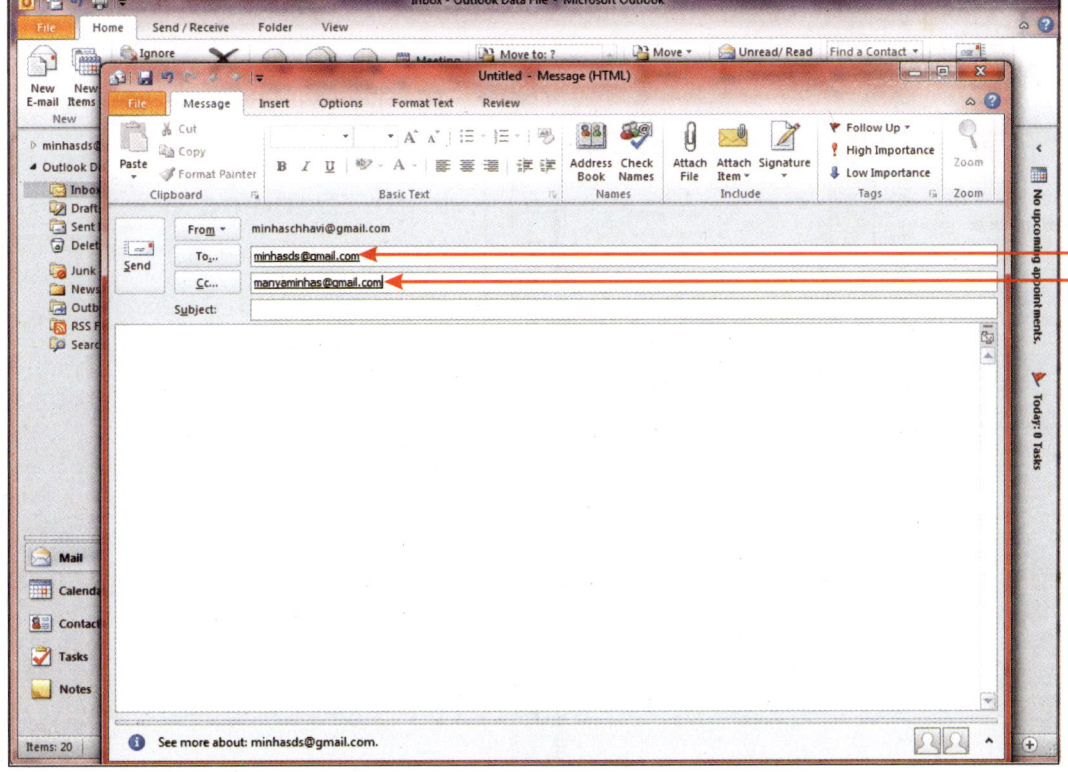

2. Type the e-mail address of the person to whom you want to send message in the **To** section.

3. If you want to send a copy of the message to a person who is not directly involved but would be interested in the message, click on **Cc** and then type the person's e-mail address.

Drag and Drop Series

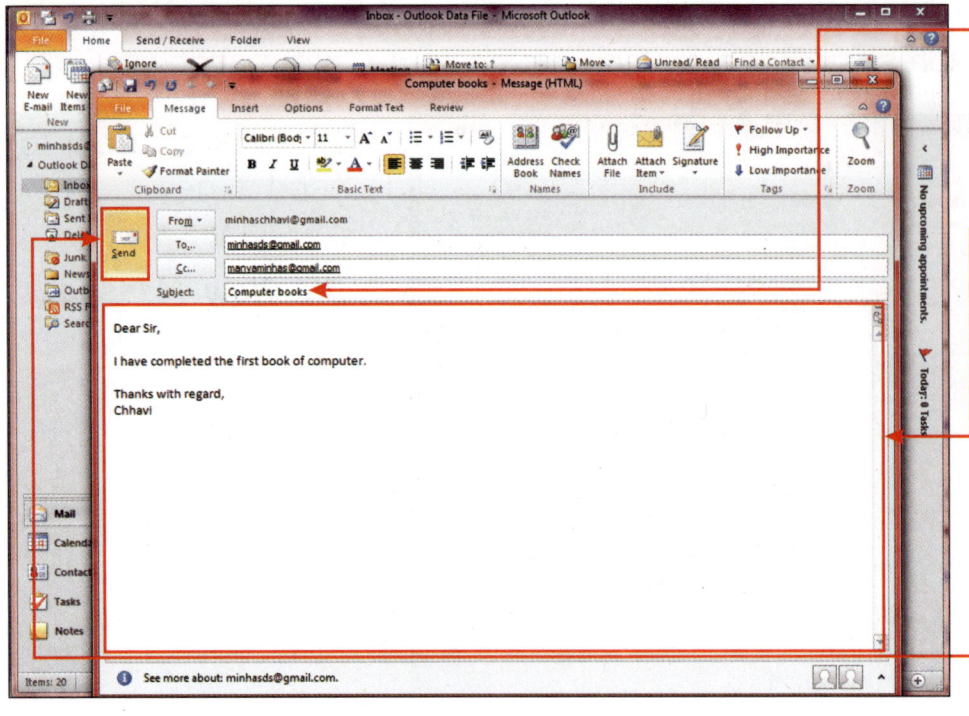

4. Click on **Subject** and then type the subject on the message.

5. Click on the message box and then type the message.

6. Click on the **Send** button to send the message.

*Outlook sends the message and stores a copy of the message in the **Sent Items** folder.*

ATTACHING A FILE TO A MESSAGE

You can attach a file to a message you are sending. Attaching a file to a message is useful when you want to include additional information with a message.

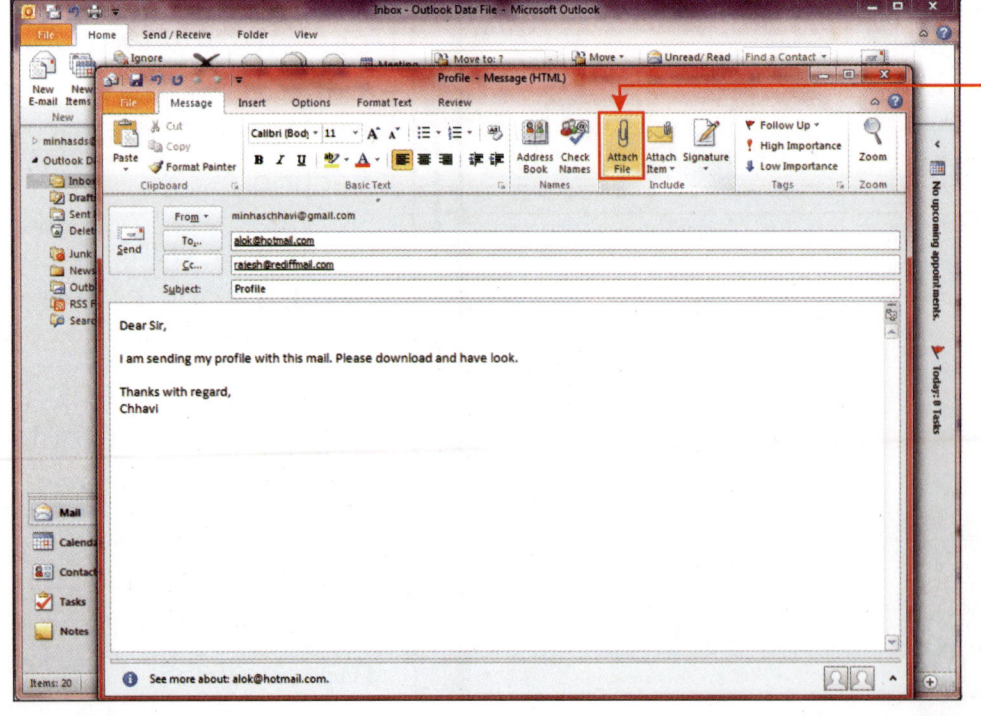

1. To create a message, perform steps **1** to **5** from "**Sending a Message**" section from the previous page.

2. Click on **Attach** to attach a file to the message.

e-mail

The **Insert File** dialog box appears.

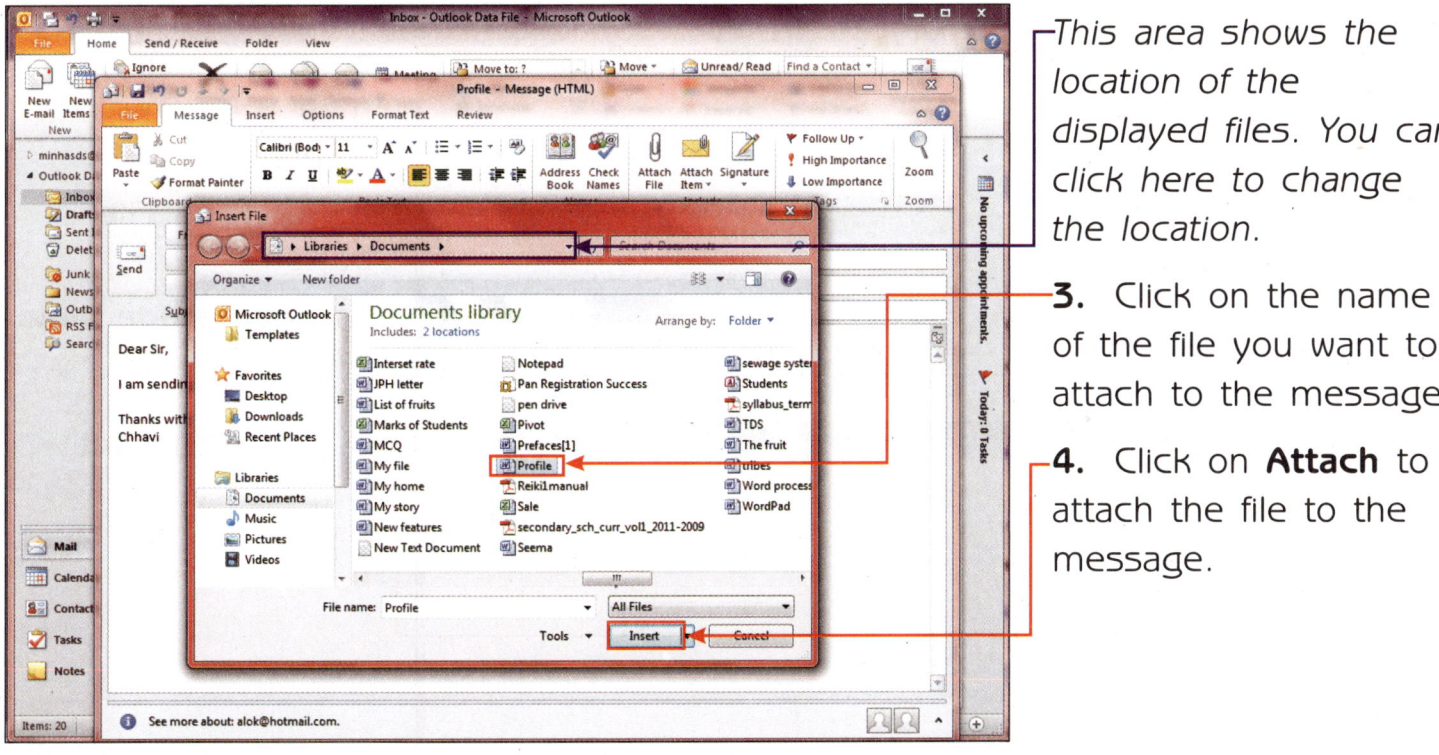

This area shows the location of the displayed files. You can click here to change the location.

3. Click on the name of the file you want to attach to the message.

4. Click on **Attach** to attach the file to the message.

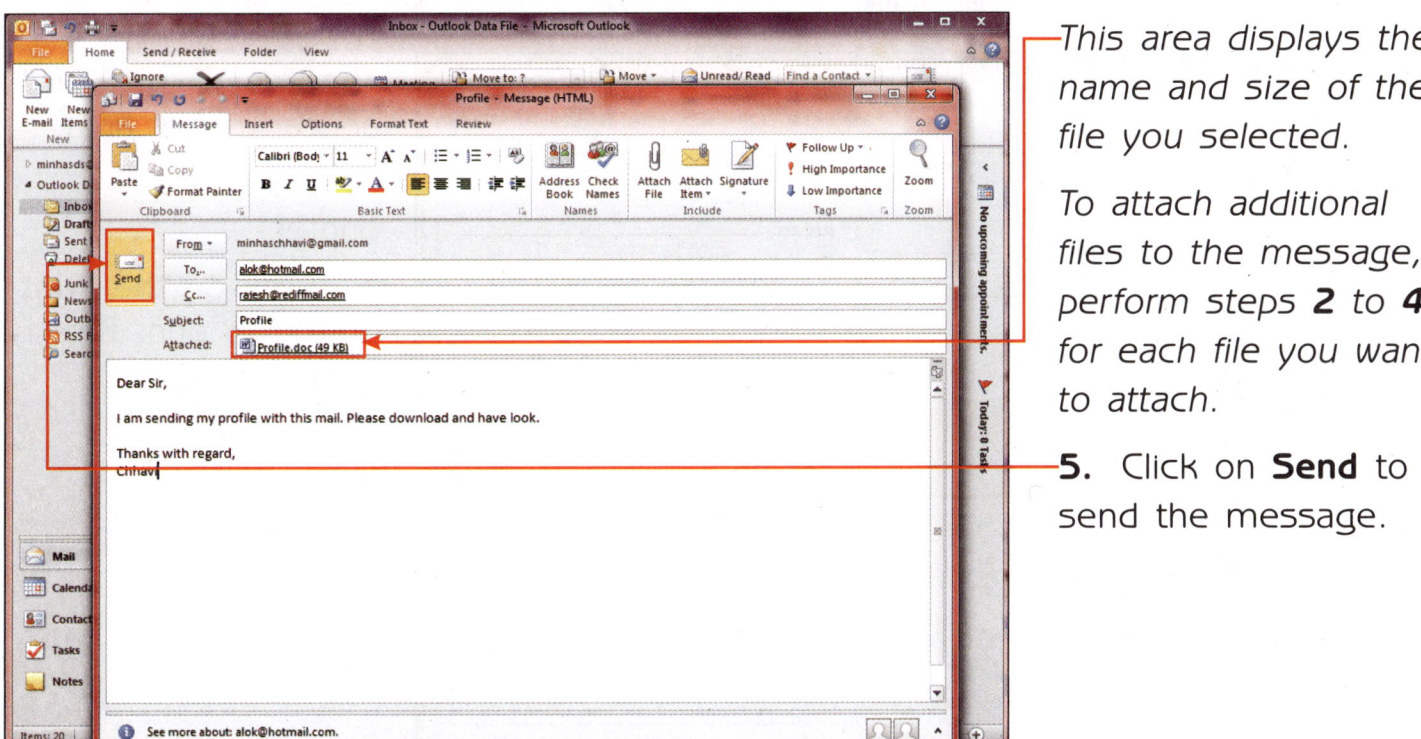

This area displays the name and size of the file you selected.

To attach additional files to the message, perform steps **2** to **4** for each file you want to attach.

5. Click on **Send** to send the message.

Outlook will send the message and the attached file(s) to the e-mail address(es) you specified.

Drag and Drop Series

PRINTING A MESSAGE

You can take the help of a printer and get a copy of your e-mail message on paper.

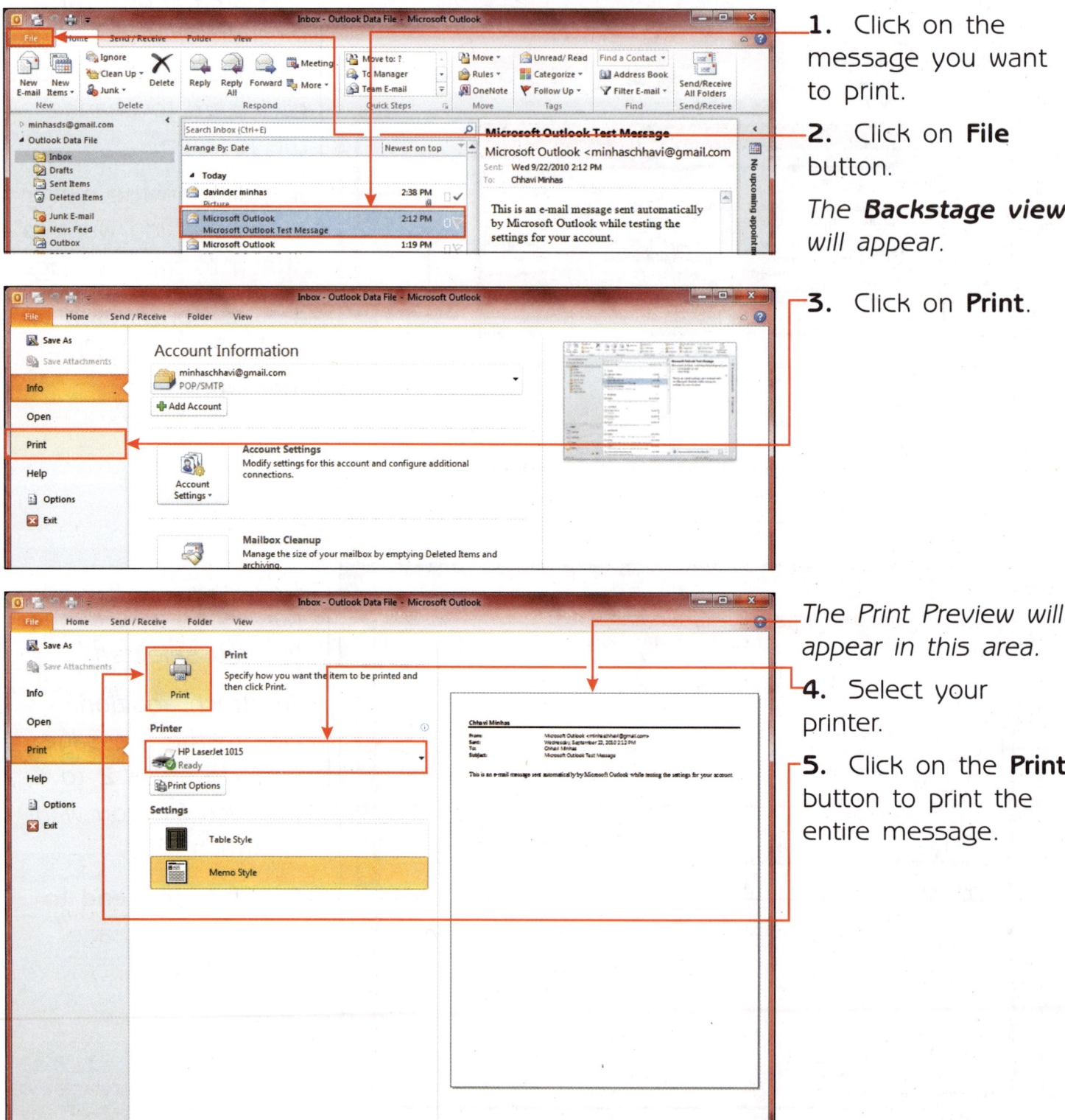

1. Click on the message you want to print.

2. Click on **File** button.

   *The **Backstage view** will appear.*

3. Click on **Print**.

   The Print Preview will appear in this area.

4. Select your printer.

5. Click on the **Print** button to print the entire message.

e-mail

DELETING A MESSAGE

You can delete a message that you no longer need.

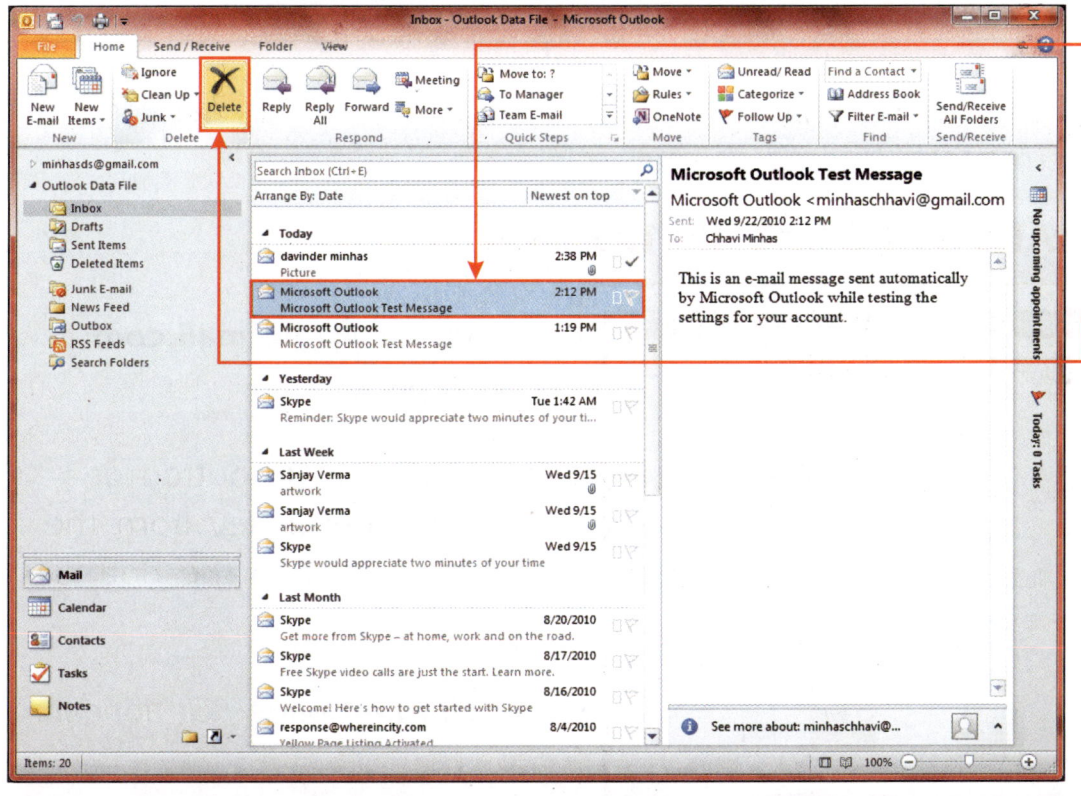

1. Click on the message you want to delete.

The message will be highlighted.

2. Click on **Delete** to delete the message.

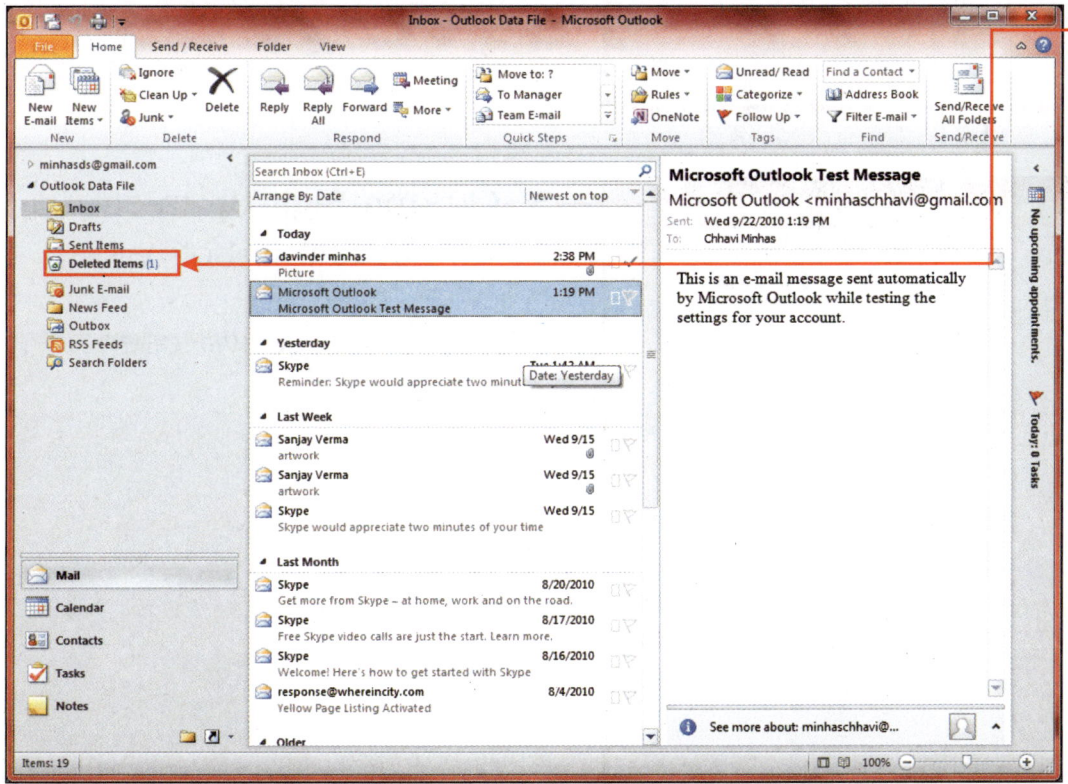

Outlook removes the message from the current folder and places the message in the **Deleted Items** folder.

*Deleting a message from the **Deleted Items** folder will permanently remove the message from your computer.*

5 Hotmail account

Hotmail is a product of Microsoft and it gives you free e-mail service that provides you with a permanent Internet e-mail address.

CREATING AN E-MAIL ACCOUNT IN HOTMAIL

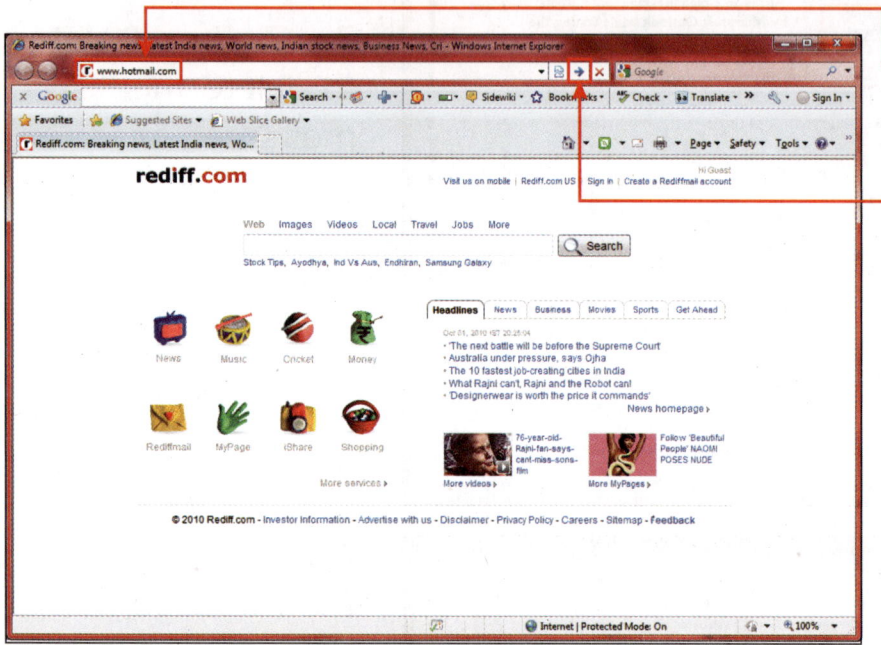

1. Type **www.hotmail.com** in your browser.

2. Press the **Go** button or press the **Enter** key from the keyboard to open the Hotmail site.

*The **Hotmail** page will appear.*

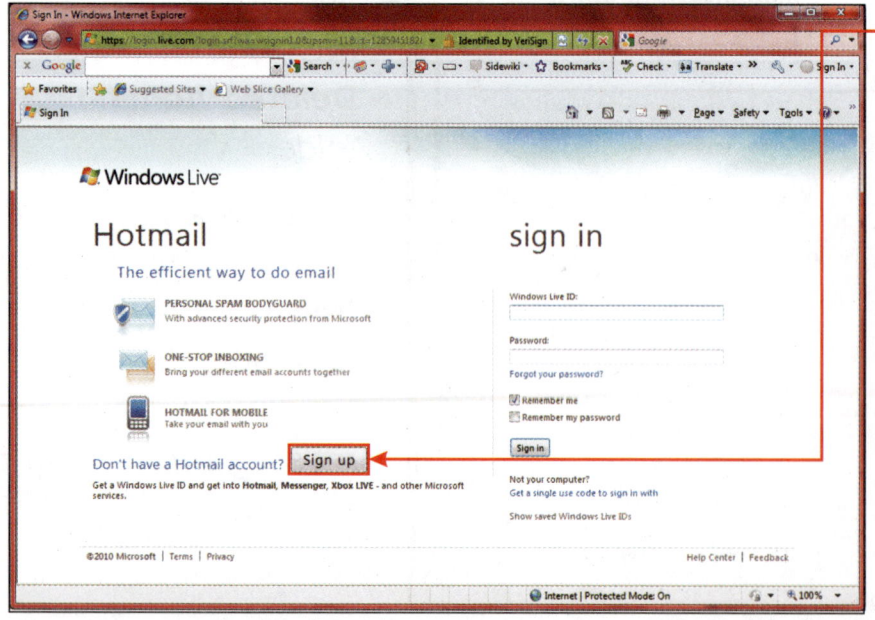

3. Click on **Sign Up** to set up a new account in Hotmail.

The Option page will open.

e-mail

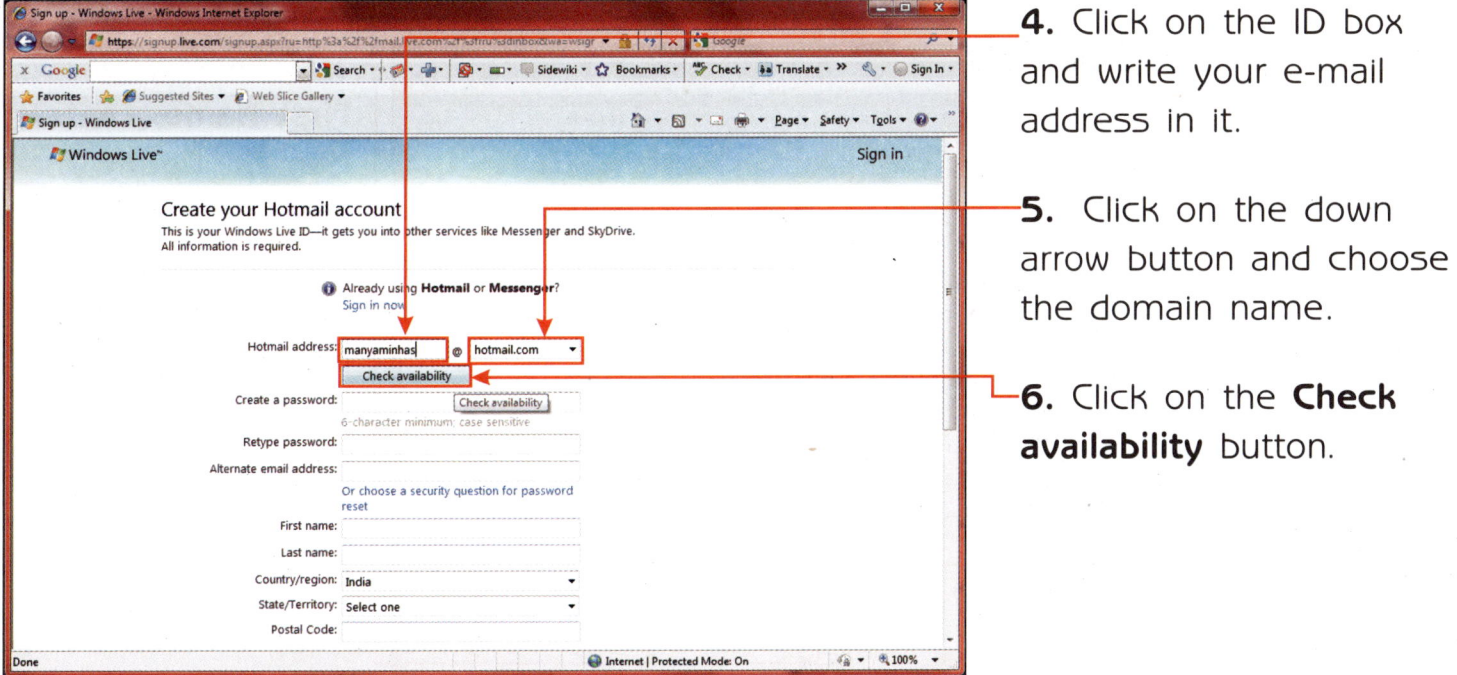

4. Click on the ID box and write your e-mail address in it.

5. Click on the down arrow button and choose the domain name.

6. Click on the **Check availability** button.

Once you click on the **Check availability** button, Hotmail checks that the e-mail address chosen by you for your e-mail account is not being used by some other person and if that e-mail address is being used by someone else, then Hotmail prompts you to re-enter some other e-mail address. If the e-mail address you choose this time is not used by somebody else, then Hotmail shows that the e-mail address chosen by you is available.

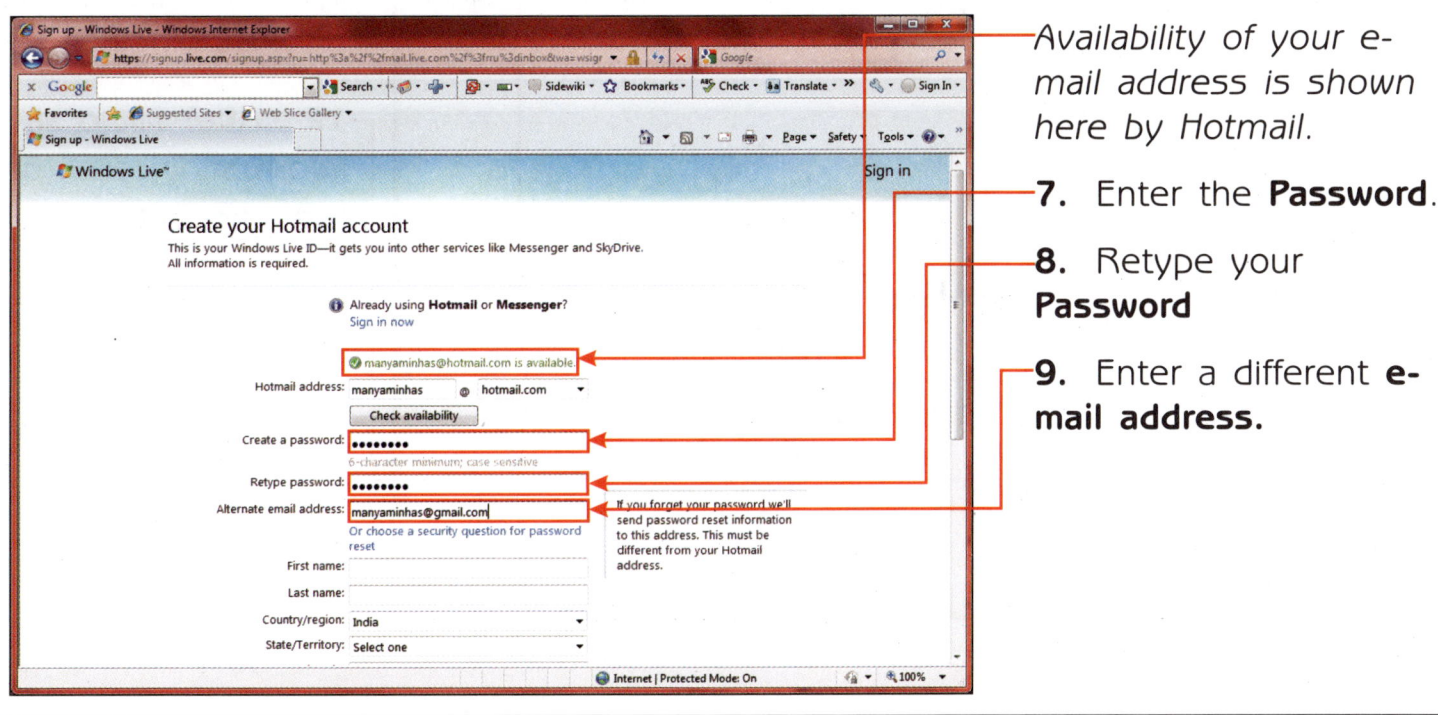

Availability of your e-mail address is shown here by Hotmail.

7. Enter the **Password**.

8. Retype your **Password**

9. Enter a different **e-mail address.**

Drag and Drop Series

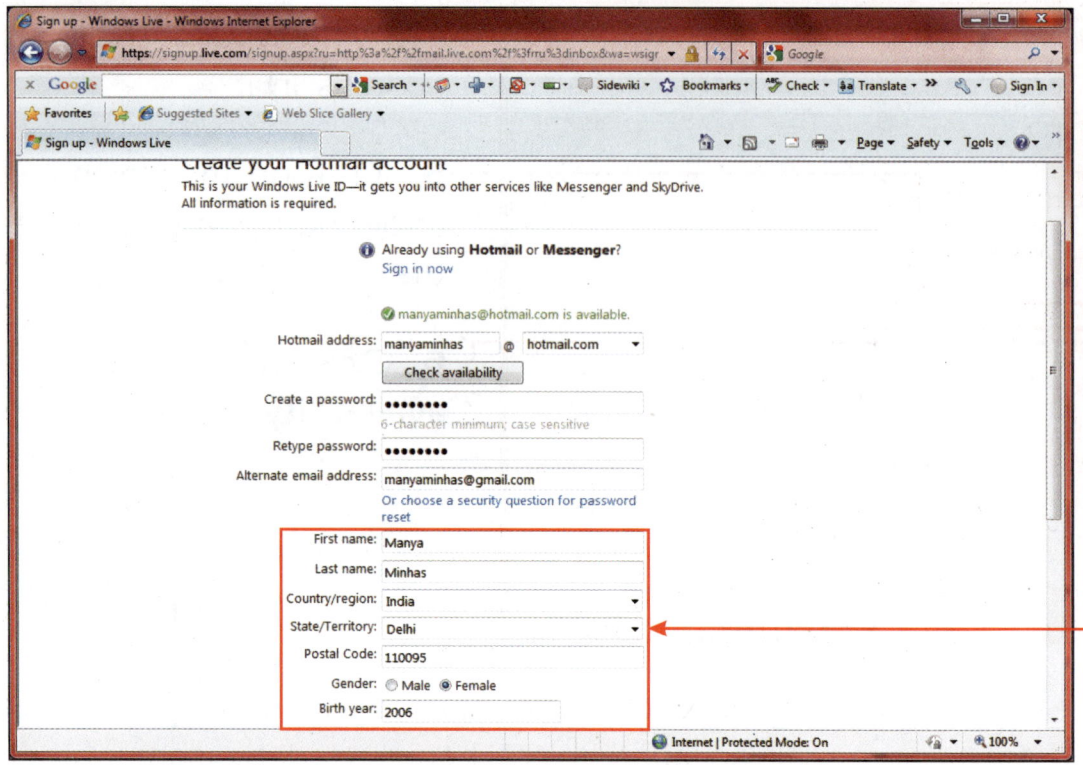

10. Enter your **First Name, Last Name, Country, State, Postal code, Gender** and **Birth year** in the information section.

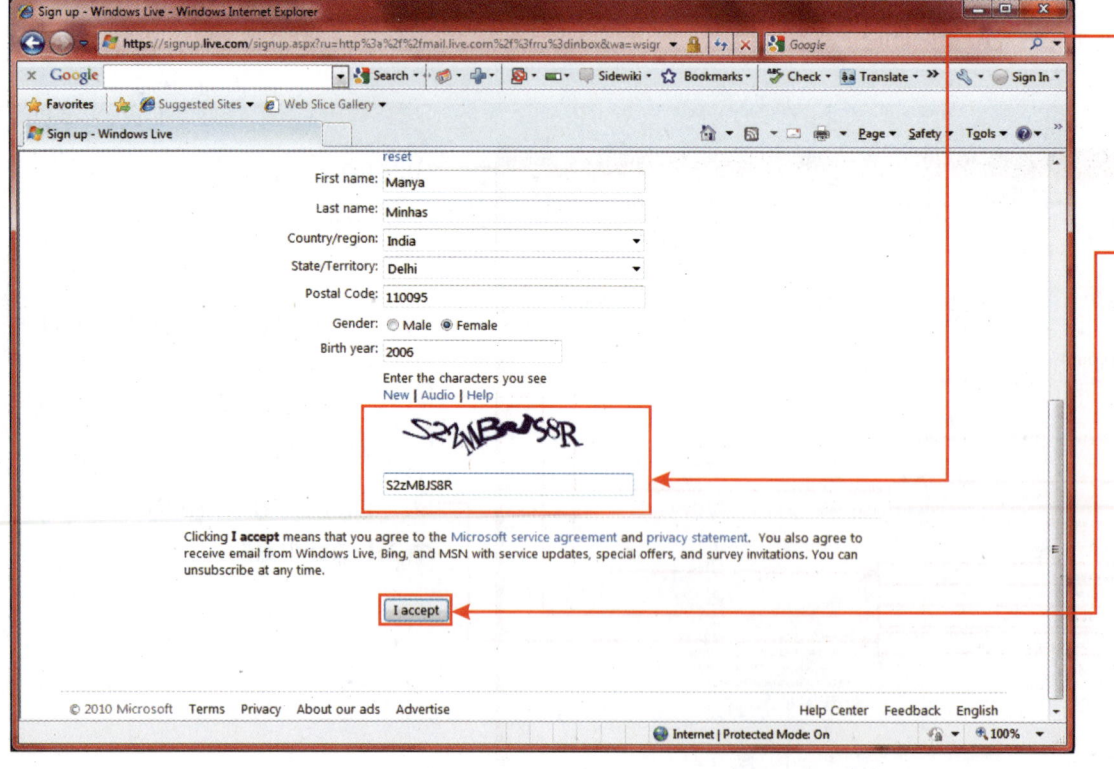

11. Type the character you see, in the picture, in the box given below.

12. After filling all information, click on the **I accept** button.

e-mail

Your account is opened and gets displayed on the Hotmail page. This page will contain your e-mail address and the mails you receive in your account.

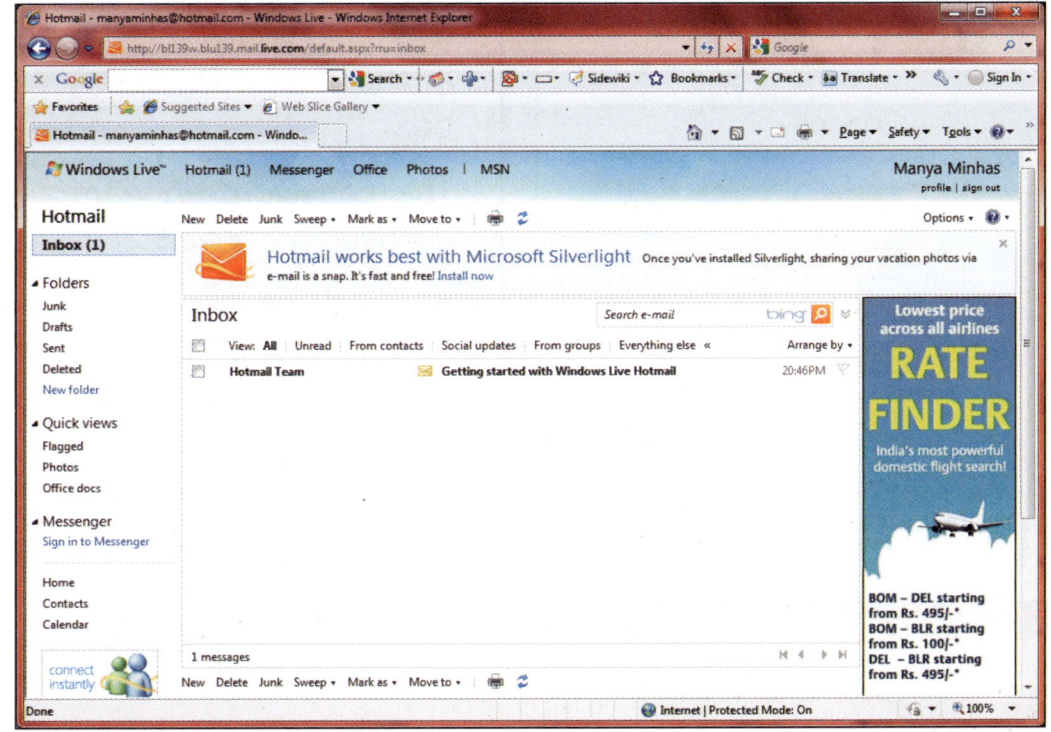

*Your **Inbox** page is displayed, which contains all the mails in your e-mail account.*

OPENING A NEW E-MAIL ACCOUNT IN HOTMAIL

After you have created your e-mail account, its time to read or send your e-mail through this program.

1. Type **http://www.hotmail.com** in this area of your browser.

2. Press the **Go** button or press the **Enter** key from keyboard to open the Hotmail site.

*The **Hotmail** page will appear.*

Drag and Drop Series

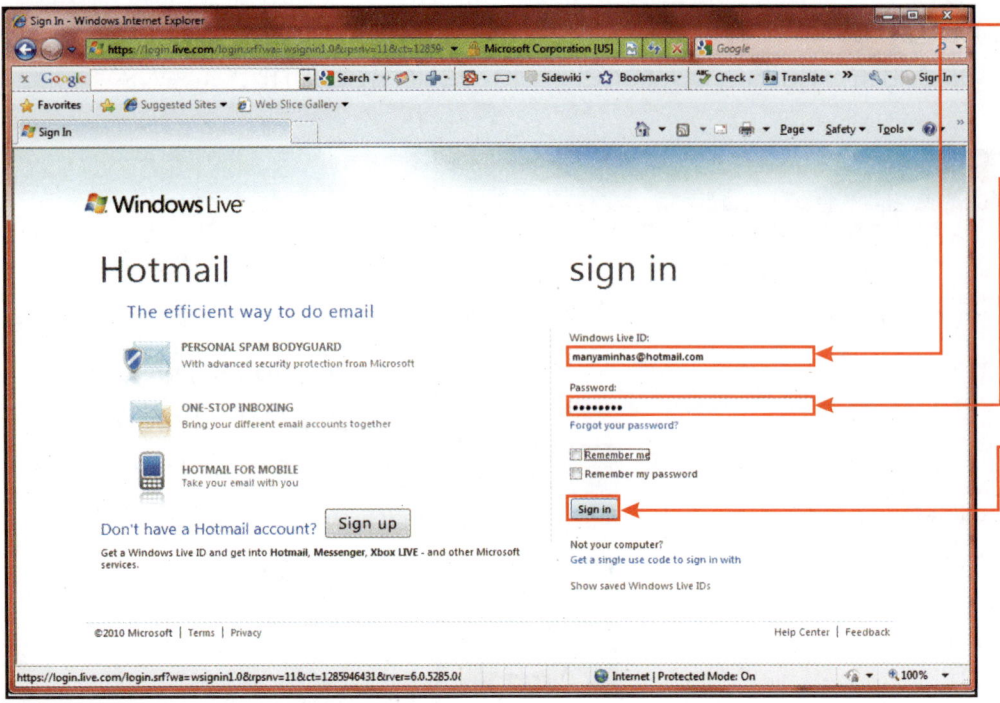

3. Type your e-mail address in the **E-mail address** text box.

4. Type your password in the **Password** text box.

   The password appears as a bullet (.) or a star (*).

5. Click on the **Sign In** button.

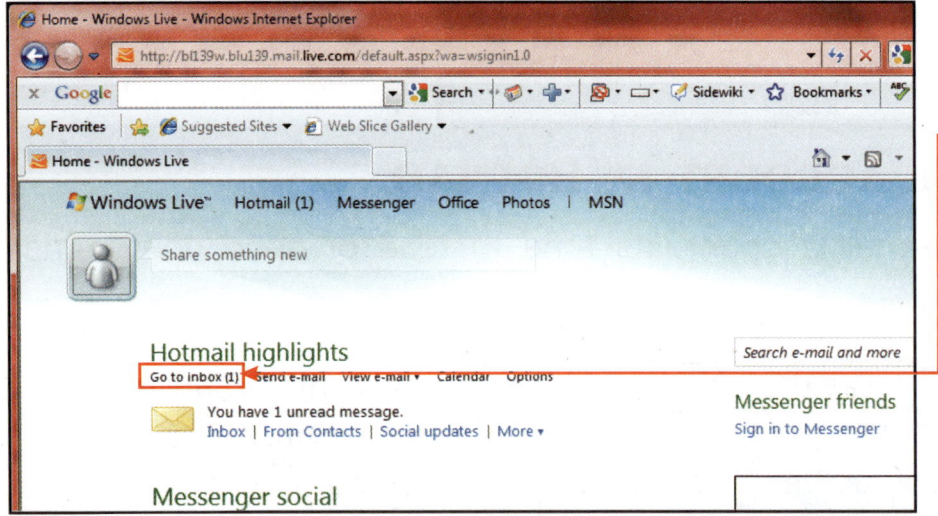

The **Hotmail** page appears with your account.

6. Click on the **Inbox** button to check your mails.

   *The **Inbox** page will appear and you can read your mail.*

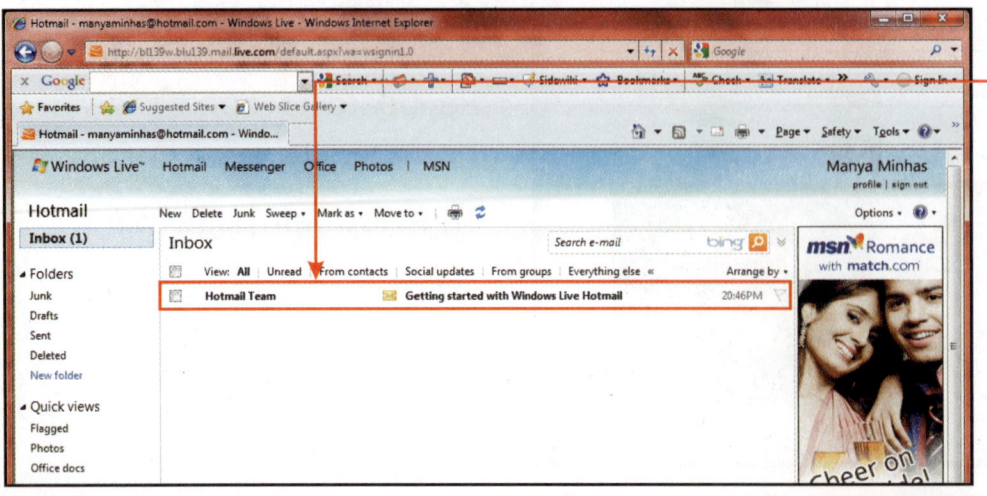

7. Click on any **mail** with the mouse pointer.

   The e-mail you selected will open.

e-mail

COMPOSE A NEW MAIL IN HOTMAIL

You can compose a mail to express your views to others.

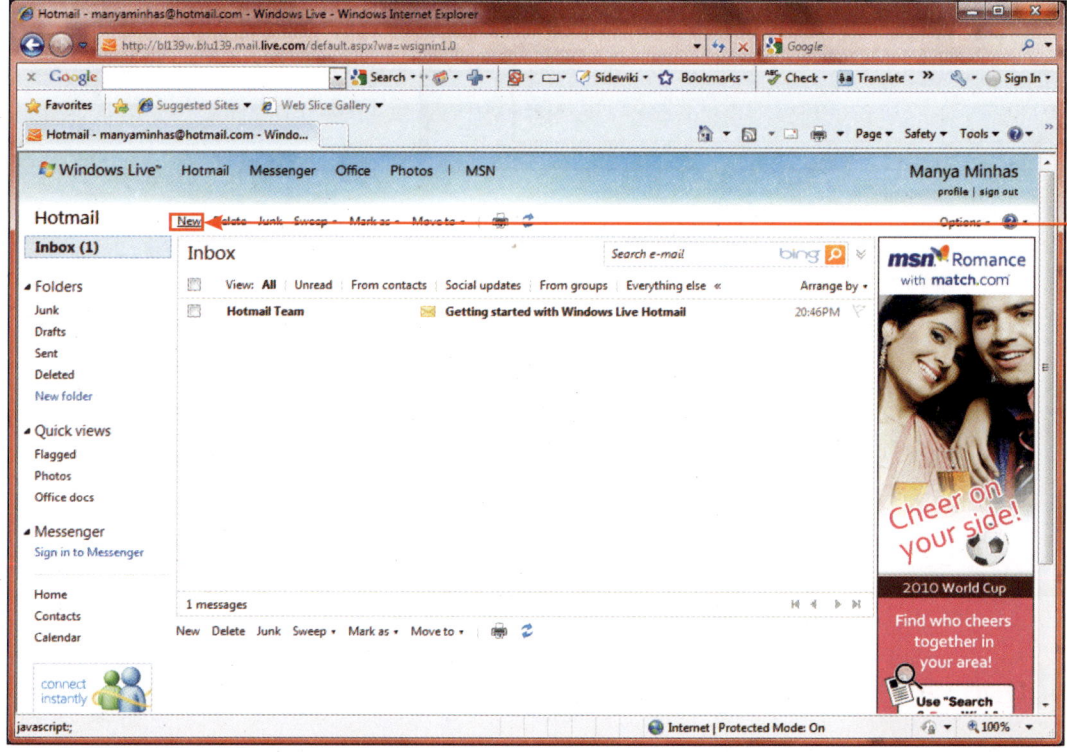

1. To compose an e-mail, first open your e-mail account by entering your user name and password.

2. Click on **New** to open a new e-mail message.

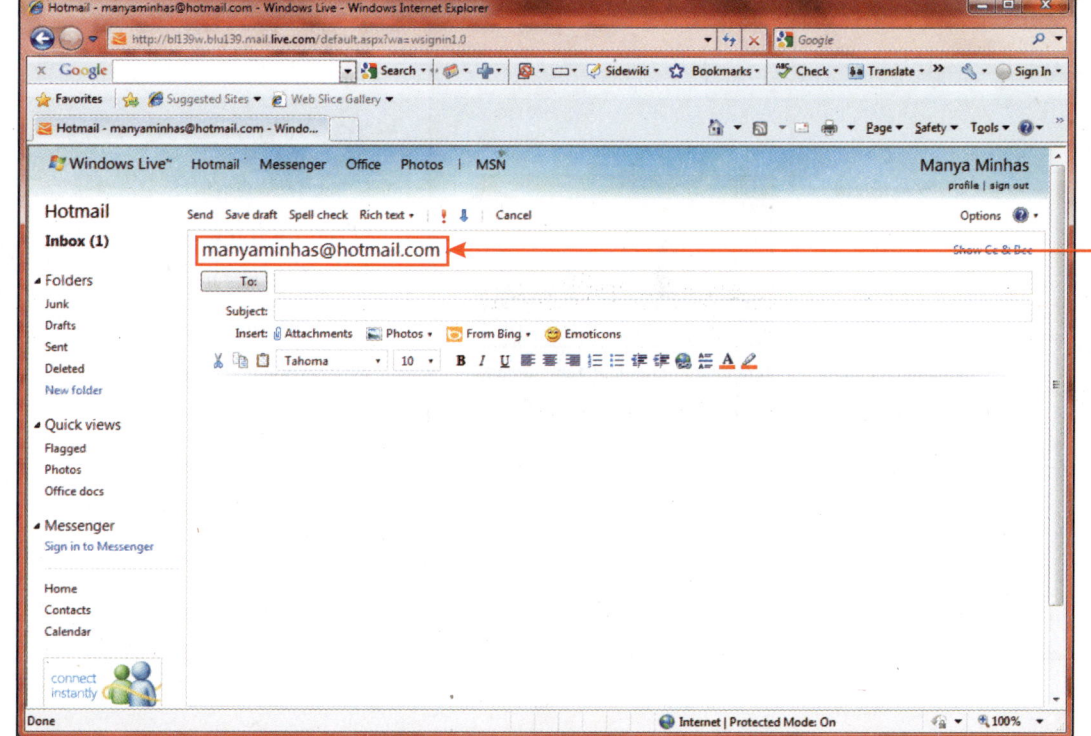

You can compose your mail in the **Compose** page.

Your e-mail address is already displayed in the **From** box.

Drag and Drop Series

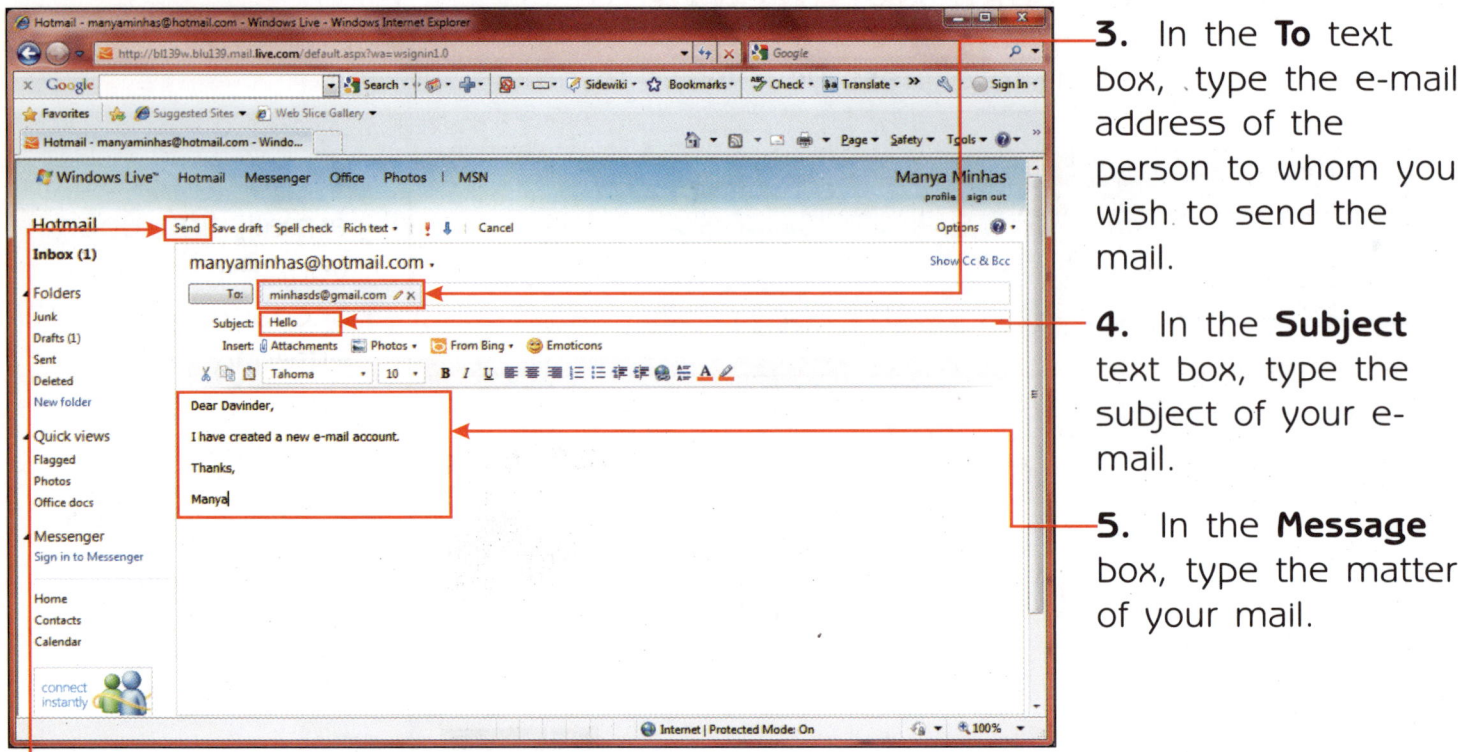

3. In the **To** text box, type the e-mail address of the person to whom you wish to send the mail.

4. In the **Subject** text box, type the subject of your e-mail.

5. In the **Message** box, type the matter of your mail.

6. Click on the **Send** button, after you have finished writing your mail.

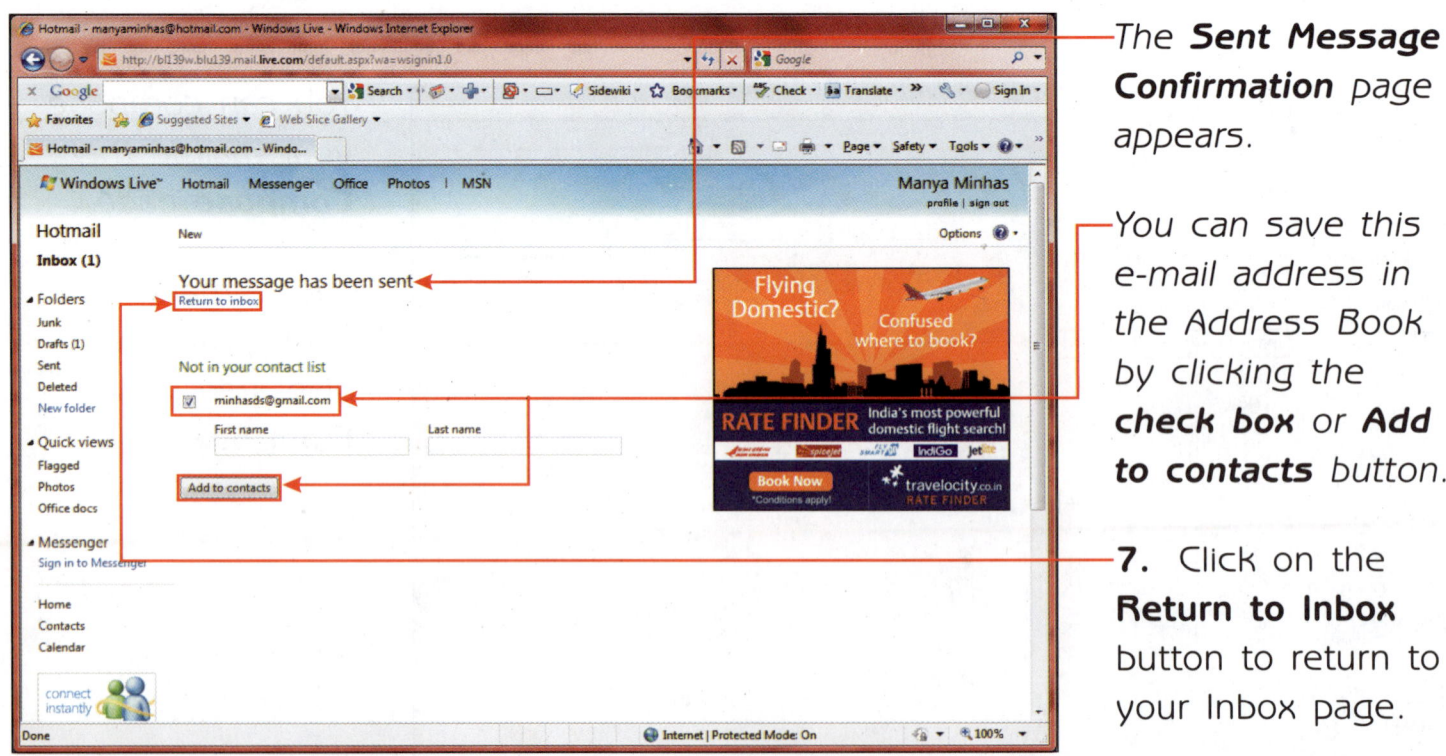

The **Sent Message Confirmation** page appears.

You can save this e-mail address in the Address Book by clicking the **check box** or **Add to contacts** button.

7. Click on the **Return to Inbox** button to return to your Inbox page.